The New Leviathans

The New Leviathans

THOUGHTS AFTER LIBERALISM

JOHN GRAY

FARRAR, STRAUS AND GIROUX
NEW YORK

Farrar, Straus and Giroux
120 Broadway, New York 10271

Grateful acknowledgment is made for permission to reprint "This is how
hunger begins . . . ," from *Russian Absurd: Selected Writings* by Daniil Kharms,
translated by Alex Cigale. Copyright © 2017 by Northwestern University Press.
Published 2017. All rights reserved.

Library of Congress Cataloging-in-Publication Data
Names: Gray, John, 1948– author.
Title: The new Leviathans : thoughts after liberalism / John Gray.
Description: First American edition. | New York : Farrar, Straus and Giroux,
    2023. | Includes bibliographical references.
Identifiers: LCCN 2023029359 | ISBN 9780374609733 (hardcover)
Subjects: LCSH: Political realism. | Nation-state. | World politics—1989–
Classification: LCC JZ1307 .G73 2023 | DDC 321/.05—dc23/eng/20230727
LC record available at https://lccn.loc.gov/2023029359

Our books may be purchased in bulk for promotional, educational, or business
use. Please contact your local bookseller or the Macmillan Corporate and
Premium Sales Department at 1-800-221-7945, extension 5442, or by
email at MacmillanSpecialMarkets@macmillan.com.

www.fsgbooks.com
www.twitter.com/fsgbooks • www.facebook.com/fsgbooks

1   3   5   7   9   10   8   6   4   2

. . . the privilege of absurdity; to which no living creature is subject, but man only. And of men, those are of all most subject to it, that profess philosophy.

Thomas Hobbes, *Leviathan*[1]

Contents

The New Leviathans

The return of Leviathan

... during the time men live without a common
power to keep them all in awe, they are in that
condition which is called war; and such a war, as is of
every man, against every man ...
In such a condition, there is no place for industry; because
the fruit thereof is uncertain: and consequently no culture of
the Earth; no navigation, nor use of the commodities that
may be imported by sea; no commodious building; no
instruments of moving, and removing such things as require
much force; no knowledge of the face of the earth; no
account of time; no arts; no letters; no society; and which is
worst of all, continual fear, and danger of violent death; and
the life of man, solitary, poor, nasty, brutish, and short.

Leviathan, Chapter 13

Twenty-first-century states are becoming Leviathans, spawn
of the biblical sea-monster mentioned in the Book of Job,
which the seventeenth-century English philosopher Thomas
Hobbes used to picture the sovereign power that alone could
bring peace to unruly humankind. Only by submitting to
unlimited government could they escape the state of nature, a
war of all against all in which no one is safe from their fellows.

As he portrayed it in his masterpiece *Leviathan*, a state of nature was not in the distant past before the emergence of society but the breakdown of society into anarchy, which could happen at any time. It did not matter whether the sovereign was a king or a president, a parliament or a tyrant. Only a state whose power was unfettered could secure a condition of 'commodious living' in which industry, science and the arts could flourish in peace.

In the centuries that followed, it seemed Hobbes was mistaken. States emerged in which power was limited by law. Democracies developed in which governments could be held to account. In the twentieth century, the defeat of Nazism and communism seemed to show that liberal government was inherently more effective than dictatorship. After the end of the Cold War, many believed liberal democracy was becoming universal.

Today, states have cast off many of the restraints of the liberal era. From being an institution that claimed to extend freedom, the state is becoming one that protects human beings from danger. Instead of a safeguard against tyranny, it offers shelter from chaos.

New dictatorships have emerged in Russia and China, where communism and free markets have both been rejected. Where democracy continues to function, the state intervenes in society to an extent unknown since the Second World War.

These are not Leviathans Hobbes would recognize. The goals of Hobbes's Leviathan were strictly limited. Beyond securing its subjects against one another and external enemies, it had no remit. The purposes of the new Leviathans are more far-reaching. In a time when the future seems profoundly uncertain, they aim to secure meaning in life for their subjects.

Like the totalitarian regimes of the twentieth century, the new Leviathans are engineers of souls.

The upshot has been the return of the state of nature in artificial forms. Even as they promise safety, the new Leviathans foster insecurity. By deploying food and energy supplies as weapons of war, Russia has projected famine and poverty across the globe. China has established a surveillance regime which through exports of technology threatens freedom in the West. Within Western societies, rival groups seek to capture the power of the state in a new war of all against all between self-defined collective identities. There is an unrelenting struggle for the control of thought and language. Enclaves of freedom persist, but a liberal civilization based on the practice of tolerance has passed into history.

In schools and universities, education inculcates conformity with the ruling progressive ideology. The arts are judged by whether they serve approved political goals. Dissidents from orthodoxies on race, gender and empire find their careers terminated and their public lives erased. This repression is not the work of governments. The ruling catechisms are formulated and enforced by civil society. Libraries, galleries and museums exclude viewpoints that are condemned as reactionary. Powers of censorship are exercised by big hi-tech corporations. Illiberal institutions are policing society and themselves.

A global pandemic, accelerating climate change and war in Europe have hastened these transformations. But they began as many historical reversals do, with the apparent triumph of an opposite trend. Greeted in the West as an augury that liberal values were spreading worldwide, the Soviet collapse was the beginning of the end for liberalism as it had previously been understood.

An epitaph for liberalism

Good, and Evil, are names that signify our appetites, and aversions, which in different tempers, customs, and doctrines of men, are different; and divers men, differ not only in their judgment, on the senses of what is pleasant, and unpleasant to the taste, smell, hearing, touch and sight; but also what is conformable, or disagreeable to reason, in the actions of common life. Nay, the same man, in diverse times, differs from himself; and one time praiseth, that is, calleth good, what another time he dispraiseth, and calleth evil: from whence arise disputes, controversies, and at last war.

Leviathan, Chapter 15

Hobbes was a liberal – the only one, perhaps, still worth reading. His best interpreters – the conservative Michael Oakeshott, the Marxist C. B. Macpherson and the classical scholar Leo Strauss[1] – all recognized him as a liberal thinker. Alone among liberals, he can help explain why the liberal experiment came to an end.

In 1986 liberalism could be defined in terms of four ideas:

Common to all variants of the liberal tradition is a definite conception, distinctively modern in character, of man and society . . . It is *individualist*, in that it asserts the moral primacy of the individual against the claims of any social collectivity; *egalitarian*, inasmuch as it confers on all men the same moral status and denies the relevance to legal or political order of differences in moral worth among human beings; *universalist*, affirming the moral unity of the human species and according a secondary importance to specific historic associations and

cultural forms; and *meliorist* in its affirmation of the corrigibil-
ity and improvability of all social institutions and political
arrangements. It is this conception of man and society which
gives liberalism a definite identity which transcends its vast
internal variety and complexity.[2]

As presented in *Leviathan* (1651) and other works, such as *De Cive*
(1642) and *Behemoth* (1681), Hobbes's political theory features all
of these ideas. Society is made up of individuals, who can assert
their claim to self-preservation against any demand by the state;
if a ruler fails to protect them, they can be disobeyed or over-
thrown. Human beings are equal in being exposed to death at
each other's hands: the strong can be killed by the weak, and no
one has a divine right to rule. Human nature is universal in its
needs; divergent cultural identities are superficial and insignificant. With the application of reason, government can be
improved. Human beings can overcome their conflicts, and
learn to live in peace.

Each of these ideas is a half-truth. Individuals may be the
basis of society; but self-preservation is only one of their needs:
bare life is not enough. Human beings may be equal in needing
protection from each other, but they regularly give up peace
and security in order to defend a form of life they believe to be
superior to others. The most basic human goods may be universal, but they are often sacrificed in order to fight for values
that are specific to particular ways of living. Society and government can be improved, but what is gained can always
be lost.

Hobbes's political theory expressed the faith in reason of the
early Enlightenment of which it was a part. His writings contain another strand in which he is not a rationalist philosopher
but a theorist of absurdity. In his account of language, he

shows how human beings allow themselves to be possessed by words. This other Hobbes can help us understand why liberal civilization has passed away.

A poor worm

He that is to govern a whole Nation, must read in himself, not this, or that particular man; but mankind . . .

Leviathan, Introduction

Hobbes has been condemned and execrated for his unsparing view of human beings. *Leviathan* was attacked as a defence of atheism and egoism, with over a hundred books being published against it in England by the end of the century in which it was published. Copies were publicly burnt by Oxford University, and Hobbes destroyed his papers to protect himself against accusations of heresy. Many of these attacks came from churchmen, for whom he was (as he said) 'a perpetual object of hatred'.

He was avoided, and at times betrayed, by fellow men of letters. The head of Oxford's Bodleian Library, who had written thanking him for the gift of a book, penned an essay arguing that Hobbes could lawfully be executed for blasphemy. A translator who had worked on rendering *Leviathan* into Latin denied he had read any of Hobbes's books and removed them from his shelves.

According to his friend John Aubrey, Hobbes

. . . had very few books. I never saw above half a dozen about him in his chamber . . . He had read much, if one considers his long life; but his contemplation was much more than his reading. He was wont to say that if he had read as much as other men, he should have known no more than other men.[3]

Intrepid in his thinking, Hobbes was timid in life. He loved routine. Aubrey described his daily habits:

> He rose about seven, had his breakfast of bread and butter; and took his walk, meditating till ten; then he did put down the minutes of his thoughts. He was never idle; his thoughts were always working . . . His dinner was provided for him exactly by eleven . . . After dinner he took a pipe of tobacco, and then threw himself immediately on his bed . . . and took a nap of about half an hour. In the afternoon he penned his morning thoughts.[4]

Aubrey comments:

> . . . it is very prodigious that neither the timorousness of his nature from his infancy, nor the decay of his vital heat in the extremity of old age, accompanied with the palsy to that violence, should not have chilled the brisk fervour and vigour of his mind which did wonderfully continue to him to his last.[5]

Hobbes was born in Westport near Malmesbury in the English county of Wiltshire on 5 April 1588, during the panic that gripped the country with news of the approaching Spanish Armada. In an autobiographical poem he described himself a as a 'poor worm', and wrote: 'My mother dear did bring forth twins at once, both me and fear.' Hobbes's father was a penurious alcoholic clergyman, who abandoned his family when Hobbes was sixteen, and died (as Aubrey writes) 'somewhere beyond London'.

Hobbes took care not to be poor, but found himself hard up at several points in his life. By choice, he did not enter a profession. Serving the Church or any institution that claimed authority over his mind was intolerable to him.

After studying at Magdalen Hall in Oxford, where he 'did not care much for logic yet he learned it, and thought himself a good disputant', he entered into the service of William Lord Cavendish, the Earl of Devonshire. Throughout much of his life he was dependent on the patronage of the Cavendish family and other aristocratic households where he lived and worked. His tasks might include private tutoring, writing letters, joining in hunting, buying horses, entertaining guests and acting as a companion. He was, in effect, a servant, but his position left him much freedom. It enabled him to explore Europe as the travelling tutor of the sons of his patrons. During his travels, he met the astronomer Galileo and many leading figures in science, literature and politics.

Hobbes's timorous twin may explain his exceptional longevity. Alarmed by what he perceived as a threat to his life in the turbulent English politics of the time, he left for Paris in 1640 – 'the first of all that fled', as he wrote with some pride – and lived in exile until 1652, a year after his most famous (and infamous) book, *Leviathan*, was published in London. Between 1646 and 1648 he was tutor in mathematics to Charles, Prince of Wales, later Charles II, when he and the future king were living in exile. After the restoration of the monarchy in 1660, he was awarded a royal pension (which the king sometimes forgot to pay) and 'free access to His Majesty, who was always delighted in his wit and smart repartees'.

Hobbes left London in 1675 and spent his remaining years with the Cavendish family on their estates. When his final illness began in October 1679 he remarked, 'I shall be glad then to find a hole to creep out of the world at.' His last words were, 'Now am I about to take my last voyage – a great leap in the dark.' He died on 4 December 1679 at the age of ninety-one.

Hobbes spent much of his life in danger. His vulnerability came partly from his supreme confidence in his own mental powers. Hobbes's prose has a lapidary finality that reflects his decisive turn of mind. An accomplished linguist, fluent in Latin, Greek, French and Italian, he was the first to write a major book of philosophy in English. His earliest published work was an English translation of Thucydides' *History of the Peloponnesian War*. Towards the end of his life he published a translation of Homer's *Odyssey* into English verse.

Though he was soaked in the classics, Hobbes had little respect for classical philosophy. He scorned Plato, Aristotle and their medieval disciples. All of them, he believed, treated words as if they were things. Imagining that abstractions conjured up by language were independently existing realities, they led the human mind into millennia of feeble self-deception.

In classical philosophy it was assumed there was a supreme good, which it was the purpose of human life to attain. Hobbes dismissed any such notion. As he wrote in Chapter 11 of *Leviathan*:

> . . . the felicity of this life, consisteth not of the repose of a mind satisfied. For there is no *finis ultimis* (utmost aim) nor *summum bonum* (greatest good,) as is spoken of in the books of the old moral philosophers. Nor can a man any more live, whose desires are at an end, than he, whose senses and imaginations are at a stand. Felicity is a continual progress of the desire, from one object to another; the attaining of the former, being still but the way to the latter. The cause whereof is, that the object of man's desire, is not to enjoy once only, and for

one instant of time; but to assure for ever, the way of his future desire . . .

So that, in the first place, I put for a general inclination of all mankind, a perpetual and restless desire of power after power, that ceaseth only in death. And the cause of this is not always that a man hopes for a more intensive delight, than he has already attained to; or that he cannot be content with a moderate power: but because he cannot assure the power and means to live well, which he hath present, without the acquisition of more.

Not love of power but fear was the primordial human passion. Values originated not in God or some spiritual realm but in the human animal. Hobbes's materialism is one reason he was denounced as an atheist. God was also material, Hobbes replied – a kind of everlasting matter. In that case, though Hobbes never admitted it, the Creator of the world pictured in the Bible was no more than a legend.

If Hobbes was an atheist, his atheism had little in common with later varieties. Believing there is no God, modern atheists attribute to humans the power to make the world according to their will that had once been assigned to the Deity. Instead, Hobbes asserted that human beings no more possess freedom of will than any other animal:

In *deliberation*, the last appetite, or aversion, immediately adhering to the action, or to the omission thereof, is that we call the will; the act, (not the faculty,) of *willing*. And beasts that have *deliberation*, must necessarily also have will . . . *Will* therefore *is the last appetite in deliberating*. (*Leviathan*, Chapter 6.)

For Hobbes, humans are like machines in that their behaviour is governed by laws of matter. But they are dreaming machines, creating imaginary worlds in their minds. In *Elements of Philosophy*, he envisioned

> . . . the world annihilated except one man to whom there would remain ideas and images of the things he had seen, or perceived by his other senses . . . though in truth they would be only ideas and phantasms internally happening and falling to the imaginant himself, nevertheless they would appear as if they were external and not dependent on the power or virtue of the mind.[6]

In Chapter 2 of *Leviathan*, he wrote in similar vein:

> . . . it is a hard matter, and by many thought impossible to distinguish exactly between sense and dreaming. For my part, when I consider, that in dreams, I do not often, nor constantly think of the same persons, places, objects, and actions that I do waking; nor remember so long a train of coherent thoughts, dreaming, as at other times; and because waking I often observe the absurdity of dreams, but never dream of the absurdities of my waking thoughts; I am well satisfied, that being awake, I know I dream not; though when I dream, I think myself awake.

Hobbes's sceptical doubts were shared by his contemporary René Descartes (1596–1650), who also recognized that waking life might be hard to tell from dreamtime. Reported to have met in 1648, they seem not to have found much in common. In Hobbes, scepticism was combined with materialism. Unlike Descartes, who posited a mind composed of a substance separate from the material world, he asserted that the mind was part of a physical body.

There was another difference. Descartes's doubt stopped with the self – as he put it, '*Cogito ergo sum*': 'I think, therefore I am.'

For Hobbes, the self was no more than a stream of thoughts and desires. Reviled for glorifying selfishness, he denied there was any such thing as the self. Human beings were like everything else, matter in motion. At the same time, inconsistently, he believed they could live rationally if they applied his philosophy.

Hobbes's faith in reason came partly from his admiration for an ancient science. Aubrey writes:

> He was forty years old before he looked on Geometry. Being in a gentleman's library, Euclid's Elements lay open . . . He read the Proposition. By G—, said he (he would now and then swear an emphatical oath by way of emphasis) this is impossible! So he reads the Demonstration of it, which referred him back to such a Proposition; which proposition he read. That referred him to another, which he also read . . . at last he was demonstratively convinced of that truth. This made him in love with Geometry.[7]

In 1655, Hobbes claimed he had solved the age-old problem of squaring the circle (constructing a square equal in area to a given circle). In some ways, his political theory was also an attempt to square the circle. If the 'state of nature' is full of mistrust, why should anyone risk making an agreement to establish an all-powerful sovereign? He never solved the problem of the first performer, who offers to keep a promise they have no reason to expect others to honour. The social contract of which Hobbes writes is a rationalist myth.

In *Leviathan*, Chapter 13, he wrote:

> . . . in the nature of man, we find three principal causes of quarrel. First, competition; secondly, diffidence; thirdly, glory.
>
> The first maketh men invade for gain; the second, for safety; and the third, for reputation. The first use violence, to make

themselves masters of other men's persons, wives, children, and cattle; the second, to defend them; the third, for trifles, as a word, a smile, a different opinion, and any other sign of undervalue, either direct or in their persons, or by reflexion in their kindred, their friends, their nation, their profession, or their name.

Hobbes knew that the causes of human conflict are tangled and at times trivial. In much of his work, though, he looks away from those that are quintessentially human. Other animals risk death for food, mates or territory, or to protect their off-spring, and some to secure dominance within a group. Only humans seek death for themselves, and inflict it on others, in order to secure meaning in their lives or vent their rage at its absence; to realize some idea through which they can achieve a spurious exemption from mortality; and on occasion to wreak death on the world out of a passion for destruction. Hobbes's pessimism is only seeming. When he asserts that self-preservation is the path to peace, he writes not as a realist but as a utopian visionary.

Seven types of absurdity

For words are wise men's counters, they do but reckon by them; but they are the money of fools, that value them by the authority of an Aristotle, a Cicero, or a Thomas, or any other doctor whatsoever, if but a man.

Leviathan, Chapter 4

Hobbes's theory of language is a key to a little-studied part of his thought. He tells us that in their use of language human beings are like God, for 'the first Author of speech was God himself, that instructed Adam how to name such creatures as he presented to his sight.' The god-like power of language separates humans from other creatures. It also instils an abiding anxiety. Humans are capable of imagining a world in which they no longer exist. Along with the power of language comes an awareness of mortality.

The ability to imagine possible futures that comes with language also brings with it the human problem of order. Other animals form packs or flocks, or cohabit – like cats – in a fluid modus vivendi. Humans exhibit no such spontaneous order. It may be natural for them to form communities, but they are always exposed to attack from other human groups. A state of nature is a peculiarly human condition.

The power of language comes with yet another consequence. As general ideas emerge, words become more real than things. In Chapter 5 of *Leviathan*, Hobbes sets out seven ways in which human beings fall into absurdity:

The first cause of absurd conclusions I ascribe to the want of method; in that they begin not their ratiocination from definitions; that is, from settled significations of their words . . .

The second cause of absurd assertions, I ascribe to the giving of names of *bodies*, to accidents; or of accidents to bodies; as they do, that say, *faith is infused*, or *inspired*; when nothing can be *poured*, or *breathed* into anything, but body . . .

The third I ascribe to the giving of names of the *accidents* of *bodies without us*, to the *accidents* of our *own bodies*; as they do that say the *colour is in the body*; *the sound is in the air*, &c.

The fourth, to the giving of the names of *bodies*, to *names*, or *speeches*; as they do that say, that *there be things universal*; that *a living creature is genus*, or *a general thing*, &c.

The fifth, to the giving of the names of *accidents*, to *names* and *speeches*; as they do that say, *the nature of a thing is its definition*; *a man's command is his will*; and the like.

The sixth, to the use of metaphors, tropes, and other rhetorical figures, instead of words proper . . .

The seventh, to names that signify nothing; but are taken up, and learned by rote from the schools, as *hypostatical*, *transubstantiate*, *eternal-now*, and the like canting of Schoolmen.

Summing up, Hobbes writes:

. . . words whereby we conceive nothing but the sound, are those we call *absurd*, *insignificant*, and *nonsense*. And therefore if a man should talk to me of a round quadrangle; or *accidents of bread in cheese*; or, *immaterial substances*; or of *a free subject*; *a free will*; or any *free*, but free from being hindered by *opposition*, I should not say he were in an error; but that his words were without meaning; that is to say, absurd.

Hobbes believed humankind could escape the spell of language by constructing clear definitions of words. Here he was misled by his rationalism. As he himself wrote, we would be wiser to use words as counters, without ever supposing that the ideas we abstract from them signify anything more than moments in the flow of thought.

The privilege of absurdity is to make sense of life through nonsense. A prime example is the word many are nowadays fond of applying to themselves. As commonly used, the idea of 'humanity' confuses 'a living creature' – the multitudinous human animal – with 'a general thing'. A species may be a useful abstraction, but when it refers to an actor in the world humanity – sometimes dignified with a capital H – is a category mistake. When people say 'we' must fight against social injustice or global warming, it is an inexistent agency they are identifying with. God is also inexistent, but no more so than Humanity. Both can only be defined by their absence.

Hobbes is not the only philosopher to have noted this confusion of categories. So did his contemporary Benedict de Spinoza (1632–77).[8] The Jewish rationalist and mystic rejected Aristotle's idea that human beings could be better or worse exemplars of humanness. All that existed were particular individuals, with some shared needs and traits but *no* ideal nature struggling to be realized.

'Humanity' is a dangerous fiction. When some human beings are identified as being less human than others, it is a small step to eliminating them. The arrival of Humanity is always preceded by mass killing.

Where the wind blows

. . . men have the liberty, of doing what their own reasons shall suggest, for the most profitable to themselves.

Leviathan, Chapter 21

Hobbes's Leviathan aimed to protect human beings from one another. Twenty-first-century Leviathans go beyond Hobbes in offering a kind of salvation. In Hobbes, Leviathan secures no meaning in life beyond what its subjects make for themselves. The new Leviathans offer meaning in material progress, the security of belonging in imaginary communities and the pleasures of persecution.

Throughout much of the twentieth century unlimited government was the chief enemy of human wellbeing.

Totalitarian states were not traditional despotisms. Old-fashioned tyrannies are like clouded leopards, a vanishing breed that kills only to feed itself. The Soviet Union, Nazi Germany and Maoist China killed in order to perfect humanity, or the part of it they judged fit to survive. Neo-totalitarian states today aim to deliver their subjects from the burdens of freedom.

The fall of Soviet communism and the shift to a market economy in China began an era of delusion in the West. Where markets spread, freedom would follow. A new world order would replace the anarchy of sovereign states. This was the theory of globalization, a mix of dubious economic theory with millennial political fantasies.[9]

Two myths supported this theory. The Austrian economist Friedrich Hayek (1899–1992), one of the most influential late-twentieth-century ideologues, believed that market capitalism spread through an evolutionary process. The most productive economic system was the free market, which would win out in Darwinian fashion over all others.

The American political theorist Francis Fukuyama invoked a different kind of evolution, sketched in the writings of the German philosopher G. W. F. Hegel (1770–1831), in which history showed one idea following another in dialectical succession. In an essay entitled 'The End of History?' published in the summer of 1989,[10] he suggested that 'democratic capitalism' would be 'the final form of human government'. The question mark in the title of the essay was dropped in his book, *The End of History and the Last Man* (1992). Here Fukuyama was following a precedent set by Sidney and Beatrice Webb, who in *Soviet Communism: A New Civilisation?*, first published in 1936, presented Stalin's totalitarian regime as a benign future for humankind. Confident that history was on their side, the once celebrated Fabian socialists removed the question mark in later editions.

The faith of liberals that their values were spreading irreversibly proved to be self-refuting. Believing they could speed this process through regime change, Western governments plunged into evangelical 'wars of choice'. With the American-led invasion in 2003, ISIS was released from the grip of Saddam's secular dictatorship and the power of Iran's theocracy increased. Toppling Muammar Gaddafi in Libya in 2011 left a stateless zone fought over by rival jihadist militias. A conclusive demonstration of Western folly came when, after twenty years of aimless occupation, American-led forces made a spectacularly squalid departure from Afghanistan in August 2021. To describe these debacles as unsuccessful exercises in democracy promotion is too charitable. None of them had any definite objectives of the kind that are required for failure.

Contrary to many of Fukuyama's critics, he did not claim liberal societies were without conflicts. He accepted that they had their own pathologies, including what later came to be recognized as a divisive kind of identity politics. Still, only democratic capitalism had a long-term future. In that sense, history – the capital 'H' history in which one idea succeeds another in a rational progression – had indeed ended. But History is like Humanity, an iridescent apparition. All that exists are mortal humans with their jarring and fading anecdotes.

In October 1989 I commented on Fukuyama's prophecy:

What we are witnessing in the Soviet Union is not the end of history, but instead its resumption – and on decidedly traditional lines.

All the evidence suggests that we are moving back into an epoch that is classically historical, and not forward into the empty, hallucinatory post-historical era projected in Fukuyama's article. Ours is an era in which political ideology, liberal as much as Marxist, has a rapidly dwindling leverage on events, and more ancient, more primordial forces, nationalist and religious, fundamentalist and soon, perhaps, Malthusian, are contesting with each other. In retrospect, it may well appear that it was the static, polarized period of ideology, the period between the end of the Second World War and the present, that was the aberration . . .

The danger for America is that confronted with comparative and soon, perhaps, absolute economic decline, an uncontrollable crime epidemic and weak or paralysed political institutions, it will drift further and further into isolation and disorder. At the worst, America faces a metamorphosis into a sort of proto-Brazil, with the status of an ineffectual regional power rather than a global superpower.[11]

The rise and fall of great powers is the normal course of history. In the 1990s, any idea that history would go on as usual was dismissed as apocalyptic. The grotesque notion that history was coming to an end in a universal convergence on American-style democracy was feted as realism.

Fukuyama joined a Hegelian philosophy of history with a Hayekian ideology of social evolution. The result was a farrago of errors and fallacies, along with occasional insights. The problem with Hegel's interpretation of history is not that it is not true but that its prognostications are consistent with almost any turn of events. Fukuyama's have at least the virtue of being false.

For Hegel, reason – human or divine, he did not specify – was unfolding in history. The conclusion of this process was the Prussian state of which he was the intellectual adornment. More modestly, Fukuyama situates the endpoint of history in the future. The triumph of liberalism was nigh, but not quite yet. In any case, history had a destination: the universal triumph of liberal values.

Here Fukuyama departs from the most important discovery in modern science. As understood by Charles Darwin, evolution has no destination. Humankind is not the endpoint of natural selection, which may well result in its extinction. As Darwin wrote in his autobiography, 'There seems to be no more design in the variability of organic beings and in the action of natural selection, than in the course in which the wind blows.'[12] (In other writings, including *The Origin of Species*, Darwin retreated from this conclusion, though it is the inexorable implication of his theory.[13])

If there is evolution in society it is like Darwin's wind. Natural selection of genes is a purposeless process that is going nowhere. Theories of social evolution, on the other hand, invariably come with a destination, which almost always embodies the values of the theorist. For the Victorian sage Herbert Spencer (1820–1903) – who coined the expression 'survival of the fittest' – the destination was laissez-faire capitalism. For Marx, who disliked Darwin's theory but believed society does evolve, it was communism. For Fukuyama, it was democratic capitalism.

Which of these anyone prefers is not very important. None of them shows any sign of arriving. As Western societies have dismantled liberal freedoms, the destination towards which the world was supposedly evolving has disappeared in the societies where it originated. There is no arc of history, short or long.

Once such fanciful notions are set aside, there is no reason to expect one mode of government to displace all others. There will be monarchies and republics, nations and empires, tyrannies and theocracies, along with many mixed regimes and stateless zones where there is no government at all. The world of the future will be like that of the past, with disparate regimes interacting with one another in a condition of global anarchy.

The seeming triumph of liberalism and the free market was not an evolutionary trend but a political experiment, which has run its course. The result has been to empower regimes in which market forces are instruments of the state.

Instead of China becoming more like the West, the West has become more like China. In both, the ruling economic system is a version of state capitalism. In each, wealth is heavily concentrated in small groups with powerful political leverage.

The exact number of billionaires in the Central Committee of the Chinese Communist party is unknown, but it is not small, and there is systemic corruption at the highest levels.[14] There may be no billionaires in the American Congress, but inequality is extremely high in the country. The US is the only advanced society in which catastrophic illness is closely correlated with personal bankruptcy. It is also one in which the rich rarely serve prison time. America's huge incarceration system is filled with the poor, the aged and ethnic minorities. China also has an enormous system of incarceration, with large numbers of inmates coming from minorities, but the rich too are at risk of confinement – or execution – if they fall afoul of the state.

In America, wealth buys power, while in China power creates and destroys wealth. In China, market forces serve the objectives of government, while Western states have ceded power to corporations that obey imperatives of profit. Both systems are variants of state capitalism, but the relations between capital and the state are reversed.

For market ideologues, Chinese companies buying up Western assets mean China is joining a Western-led liberal order. For China, such acquisitions are means through which the West can be colonized. When enterprises controlled by the Chinese state invested in British nuclear power stations, they acquired an asset they could deploy in geopolitical conflict. When companies like Apple and Tesla invest in China, they give hostages to a strategic rival. In its competition with China, Western capitalism is programmed to fail. Only if China's leaders make major mistakes can the West hope to prevail.

If an evolutionary process is at work, there is no reason to think it favours the West. Evolution is natural selection among random mutations. The regimes that prevail will be those that best adapt to the random walk of history. Not the most productive societies but those that best exploit opportunities thrown up by chance are the fittest.

While history is not the unfolding of reason, there can be logic in particular situations. The contest between two kinds of state capitalism may be one such juncture. Systems in which market forces are directed by the state have an inherent advantage over ones in which government has been captured by corporate power.

Western economists insist China's state capitalism is bound to lack innovation. Economic growth in China is slowing due to rising debt and environmental pollution. Demographic imbalances resulting from the one-child policy mean the country is growing old faster than it is becoming richer. Xi's Zero Covid policy did incalculable damage. The days when the Chinese economy seemed an invincible juggernaut are over.

That does not mean China must lag in science and technology. It is outpacing the West in areas such as robotics, quantum computing, virtual reality and weapons systems. For many in Washington, derailing China's advance is the strategic imperative of the age. Blocking China's access to Western advanced microchip technology, Biden's Chip Act of August 2022 was effectively a declaration of economic war. The danger is that it will provoke pre-emptive military action, as America's oil blockade of Japan did at Pearl Harbor in December 1941. This time, America may not prevail.

A naval war in the Taiwan Straits might resemble the Battle of Tsushima in 1905, when the Japanese Imperial Navy sank almost the entire Russian Imperial Pacific fleet. Russia's defeat served as an early warning of the fragility of the tsarist empire. Defeat by China could have a similar impact on American power. In the event, the US – with its heavy reliance on China for medical supplies and financing the federal deficit, its offshoring of industrial production to the Chinese mainland and its introverted culture wars – may retreat from any military confrontation.

That does not mean America will hand supremacy to China. India will not accept such an outcome; nor, probably, will Japan. The upshot of the struggle for hegemony will be a world with no hegemonic power.

Russia's Orthodox Leviathan

The darkest part of the kingdom of Satan, is that which is without the Church of God ... We are therefore yet in the dark.

Leviathan, Chapter 44

Many Western observers were surprised when, in a speech to leaders of the country's armed forces, Patriarch Kirill of Moscow and all Russia gave the blessing of the Russian Orthodox Church to Putin's invasion of Ukraine when it was launched on 24 February 2022. Congratulating Putin on his service to Russia, the Patriarch praised the military as 'the active manifestation of evangelical love for neighbours'. In October 2022, Kirill conferred on Putin the titles of 'fighter against the Antichrist' and 'chief exorcist'. Aleksey Pavlov, assistant secretary of the Security Council of the Russian Federation, was reported by the Russian state news agency, Tass, as having described the aim of Putin's 'special military operation' as 'de-satanization'.[15]

Western puzzlement reflected a long-standing failure to understand the role of religion in the Russian state. Expanding their power when the Soviet Union fell apart, the security services reached deeply into the Russian Orthodox Church (ROC). The subservience of the Church to the state, which existed under tsarism and throughout the Soviet period, increased in the post-communist era.

A stupefying cliché has it that Putin became a new tsar. In fact he never achieved the legitimacy the tsars possessed at their worst. For a time he may have been popular as a pragmatic authoritarian who presided over a period of relative freedom and prosperity. But his authority was always precarious, resting on a coalition of organized crime and the security services that had no precedent in the Romanov despotism that endured for 300 years.

If Putin has an ideology, it is a version of Eurasianism, in which Russia is a civilization apart from the West. Most likely created by the Bolshevik security services to entice the Russian diaspora into supporting the Soviet regime, the Eurasian movement first appeared among the émigré Russian intelligentsia in the 1920s. In recent times Eurasian ideology was revived by the political theorist Alexander Dugin. It is unclear whether Dugin ever advised Putin, but Dugin's daughter was killed in August 2022 during an alleged Ukrainian assassination attempt on him as a Putin ally.

Putin flirted with Eurasianism as part of rejecting the influence of the West, but the state he built was founded on a Western model. The Russian security services are successors of the Cheka, the secret police founded by Lenin in December 1917, which replicated the French Reign of Terror of 1793–4 on a larger scale. For Lenin, as for the Jacobin leader Maximilien Robespierre (1758–94), the chief purpose of terror was to eradicate the false consciousness of the people.

The FSB, the successor to the KGB and the Cheka, forms the skeleton of the twenty-first-century Russian state. Many believe Bolshevik totalitarianism was little more than an extension of tsarist autocracy. There are continuities, but a comparison of the tsarist and Bolshevik security services reveals a radical disjunction. Whereas the Romanov empire was a traditional despotism, the Soviet state was a new Leviathan, unlike Hobbes's in aiming to fashion a new humanity. That is one reason why the Soviet security service soon became far larger, and had a much more invasive presence in society, than that of the tsars.

In 1895 the Okhrana – the tsarist secret service – had 161 full-time personnel. By 1916 the number had increased to around 15,000. The tsarist regime colluded in extra-legal violence, including atrocious pogroms. (As Isaac Babel reported in the diary he wrote of his time serving in the Red Cavalry during the Russian Civil War, allies of the Bolsheviks also committed atrocities against Jews.[16]) But the Okhrana was not an instrument of social engineering, while the Cheka was explicitly founded to create a new kind of society.

Lenin's secret police increased from twenty-three operatives in December 1917 to no fewer than 37,000 in 1919. By 1921 it consisted of around a quarter of a million. The casualties of the Soviet regime between 1917 and 1924 were larger than all those of the last half-century of tsarism added together.[17] In the fifty years from 1867 to 1917, there were around 25,000 deaths from executions and pogroms. In the first five years of the Soviet state's existence, there were around 200,000 executions by the Cheka, a figure that takes no account of deaths in camps or casualties in the Russian Civil War.[18]

The Soviet Union was a totalitarian project from the start. A state of this kind uses violence and terror not only in order to quash opponents, as despots have always done, but to remodel its subjects. As a historian of the KGB has written:

Prior to the appearance of the Soviet party–state, history offered few, if any, precedents of a millenarian, security-focused system. One might argue that the generic 'Oriental' or 'Asiatic' despotisms studied by such disparate students of social history as Karl Marx, Max Weber, or Karl Wittfogel presented compelling analogies for such a system. However, certain key ingredients (such as an all-embracing, ubiquitous ideology or a continuously institutionalized secret police) were lacking in those despotisms both in scope and intensity. Certainly, intrusive claims on the totality of human existence, common to the Soviet state, were not characteristic of those despotisms.

The Bolshevik victory created a party–state structure that equated domestic opposition (and later, even apathy) with treason; declared whole classes of people as foreordained by history to destruction; and arrogated to itself a mandate to execute history's will on an international scale . . . In a sense, a secular theocracy was born in which a priesthood (the party), served by a combined holy office and temple guard (the Cheka), sought to exercise its will: the imposition of its ideas and the elimination of those actually or potentially opposed.[19]

After the communist party left government, any institution that could rival the power of the KGB and its successors disappeared. The security services had always been a state within a state. Now they became the state itself. In a parallel development, the role of the Church in the state became stronger. Writing in the early 1990s, an astute Russian observer noted: 'the Russian Orthodox Church has of late come to occupy the ideological niche filled until recently by the Communist Party.'[20]

The penetration of the Church by intelligence operatives goes back to the beginnings of the Soviet regime. A minute of a meeting of the Cheka in 1921 emphasized the need to 'use the clergy for our own purposes, especially those who occupy an important position in Church life, for example bishops or metropolitans, forcing them under fear of severe consequences . . . Material incentive for a clerical informer is essential . . . Recruitment of informers must also proceed through threat of prison and labour camp.'[21]

The recruitment of clergy was reaffirmed in a KGB directive in July 1970. Patriarch Alexey II of Moscow and all Russia, the first post-Soviet primate of the Russian Orthodox Church and the predecessor of the current Patriarch Kirill, was a KGB agent recruited in 1958.[22] The young Kirill himself has been reported to have been an agent on the basis of material recovered from KGB archives.[23]

When Kirill blessed the invasion of Ukraine, he was offering a theological justification for a claim made by Putin in a 5,000-word essay, 'On the Historical Unity of Russians and Ukrainians', published in July 2021. (Kirill's stance on the invasion provoked opposition from within Orthodoxy, with churchmen in Ukraine and other countries going so far as to support a split from the Moscow Patriarchate. Some Orthodox clergy in Russia have also dissented.) In the essay and a two-hour televised address before the invasion, Putin asserted that Ukraine belonged in *'Russky mir'*, 'the Russian world', a realm that included Belarus, Moldova, parts of the Baltic states and possibly Kazakhstan. The origins of this realm were in the conversion of Vladimir the Great, the Grand Prince of Kyiv, who began the Christianization of Russia in the tenth century. In this semi-mystical vision, Moscow and Kyiv are the temporal and spiritual centres of a single state.

Putin's essay continued a mythology of Russia as 'a Third Rome', charged with the task of redeeming the sinful West, which reaches back many centuries. The Russian Orthodox philosopher Nicolai Berdyaev (1874–1948) described this tradition:

> After the fall of the Byzantine Empire, the Second Rome, the greatest Orthodox state in the world, there awoke in the Russian people the consciousness that the Russian Muscovite state was left as the only Orthodox state in the world and that the Russian people was the only nation who professed the Orthodox Faith . . .
>
> The doctrine of Moscow the Third Rome became the basic idea on which the Muscovite state was formed. The kingdom was consolidated and shaped under the symbol of a messianic idea . . . The Moscow Orthodox kingdom was a totalitarian state.[24]

Berdyaev linked Muscovite messianism with the Bolshevik revolution:

> . . . the meaning of revolution is an inward apocalypse of history. Apocalypse is not only a revelation of the end of the world and of the last judgment. Apocalypse is also the revelation of the continual nearness of the end within history itself . . . of a judgment upon history within history itself, an exposure of its failure.[25]

Berdyaev provides a profound analysis of the cultural origins of the Russian Revolution. Born into a noble military family, he was the maternal great-grandson of a French nobleman forced to flee to Russia during the Reign of Terror in 1793. The Bolshevik Revolution forced Berdyaev to flee the other way. He arrived in France in 1924 after having been deported from Russia in 1922, along with other intellectuals and cultural figures, on a steamship chartered by Lenin. Prior to his expulsion, Berdyaev clashed with the head of the Cheka, Felix Dzerzhinsky, who visited him in gaol after he was arrested on charges of conspiracy. Before the revolution, he had been accused of blasphemy for criticizing Church elders, but the case was never tried.

In exile in Paris, Berdyaev declined to join any of the groups founded to promote Orthodoxy, because they would fetter his freedom of thought.[26] He was fearless in denouncing émigrés who refused to accept responsibility for the collapse of tsarism.[27] When a member of the audience at a talk he gave in Paris claimed Jews had engineered it, Berdyaev silenced the speaker with a thunderous command to leave the meeting, which he did.

Berdyaev believed Russian communism was religious in nature: 'Russian atheism, in its most profound forms, may be expressed in the following paradox: God must be denied, in order that the Kingdom of God may come on earth.'[28] It should not be surprising that when the communist secular theocracy collapsed it was followed, under Putin, by a more authentically theocratic regime. Vyacheslav Nikonov, Deputy Head of the State Duma, declared on 18 April 2022, 'This is a metaphysical clash between the forces of good and evil . . . This is truly a holy war we're waging and we must win.'[29]

But the theocratization of the Russian state had been underway for a generation. Beginning in the Yeltsin era, the ROC became part of core government institutions, particularly the armed forces. It has become embedded in the nuclear weapons complex, where theories of deterrence based on rational calculations of survival coexist with eschatological ideas of a world-destroying apocalypse.

Apocalyptic language has featured in several of Putin's public pronouncements. In March 2018, addressing the Russian Federal Assembly, Putin said: 'As a citizen of Russia and head of the Russian state, I must ask myself: "Why would we want a world without Russia?" '[30] In October 2018, speaking at the Valdai Discussion Club, he mused: 'Aggressors will be annihilated. We will go to heaven as martyrs, and they will just drop dead.'[31]

In the post-Soviet Leviathan, Orthodoxy

. . . saturated the Russian military-industrial complex. Each leg of the nuclear triad (army, navy and air-force) has its patron saint, and their icons hang on the walls of the consecrated headquarters and command posts. Icons appear on the nuclear platforms; aerial, naval and ground processions of the cross are routine; the military clergy provide regular pastoral care to the nuclear corps' servicemen . . . Within each big base there is a garrison church, chapel or prayer room. The nuclear priest-hood and commanders jointly celebrate religious and professional holidays, and catechization is an integral part of the military and civilian higher nuclear education. A similar situation prevails within the nuclear industry.

Supplication services and the sprinkling of holy water occur during parades, the oath of allegiance, exercises, manoeuvers, space and nuclear launches, and combat duties. Nuclear priests are integrated into professional activities through the whole chain of command and join their flock during operational missions on the ground and underwater. Pilots of strategic bombers consecrate their jets before combat sorties, and icons are attached to the maps they take to the cockpit. Mobile temples accompany intercontinental ballistic missiles, and nuclear submarines have their portable churches. Within the Russian military, in particular within the nuclear forces, the scope and frequency of clerical activities fostering patriotism, morale and human rehabilitation have made the priests almost equivalent to Soviet-era political officers. History has come full circle. In the Soviet era 'red corners' were located in public places to present an iconostasis of the new saints of Marxism-Leninism, replacing the Orthodox icons. Now, the new mythology and iconography have replaced the Soviet icono-stasis with a new-old one, in which traditional Russian and newly canonized saints and warriors from Russian and Soviet history harmoniously coexist . . . The Russian Orthodox Church has positioned itself as one of the main guardians of the state's nuclear potential and, as such, claims the role of one of the main guarantors of Russian national security.[32]

In 2007, during an annual presidential press conference, Putin linked Orthodoxy and nuclear weapons, remarking:

'Traditional confessions and the nuclear shield are components that strengthen Russian statehood and create the necessary conditions for providing the state's internal and external security.'[33] Putin's formula was cited in the mass media, with one journalist summarizing it approvingly: 'Nuclear Orthodoxy is an eschatological Russian strategy for all time.'[34]

Many have questioned Putin's Orthodox beliefs. His religiosity could be an application of the 'political technology' associated with former advisers such as Vladislav Surkov, who blended Bolshevik strategies of deception with 'post-modern' techniques for shaping perception.[35] Putin's faith may be a media legend, confected for political purposes.

Born in 1952 in a still half-destroyed Leningrad into a working-class family, with a father badly injured in the war and a mother who nearly starved in the German blockade, Putin fought with rats that infested his apartment block and joined street gangs that surrounded it. In interviews he has claimed to have been secretly baptized as a baby at his mother's request by the father of Patriarch Kirill. When he travelled to Israel in 1993 as part of a delegation from the Leningrad city council, his mother asked him to consecrate his baptism cross in the Church of the Holy Sepulchre in Jerusalem. Putin did not wear a cross before his visit, but since fulfilling his mother's request he appears not to have taken it off. He had house chapels built for his personal use in the Kremlin and at his private residence at Valdai. If Putin's faith is a deception, it goes back a long way.[36]

Berdyaev writes that 'Russian thought is essentially eschatological,'[37] but this is in part because of the country's singular history, in which the sudden evanescence of a human world has been a recurrent experience. If the passing of tsarism ended one world, the Civil War buried it. An assault on civilian populations more destructive than any conflict in European history since the Thirty Years War, it included the deaths of up to twelve million people in mass slaughter and huge pogroms, the near destruction of the economy and plagues of cholera and other diseases. In some famine-struck regions, cannibalism showed itself in public markets in human flesh, with prices varying according to whether the bodies were newly killed or retrieved after death.[38] The war itself was horribly cruel. As a definitive history concludes: 'All too often the Whites represented the worst examples of humanity. For ruthless inhumanity, however, the Bolsheviks were unbeatable.'[39]

The Bolsheviks used violence to liquidate social groups that had no place in the new world they were building. The emergence of a new human type required the systematic severing of human beings from their cultural roots. A new kind of human being did emerge, but it was the opposite of that which the Soviet state meant to create.

The Polish author Ryszard Kapuściński described this process:

This ethnic *Homo Sovieticus* is a product of the history of the USSR, a significant portion of which comprises unceasing, intense and massive migrations, displacements, transportations, and wanderings of the population. This movement begins in the nineteenth century with the deportations to and colonization of Siberia, as well as the colonial expansion into Asia, but it gathers strength only after 1917. Millions of people lose the roof over their head and spill out onto the roads. Some are returning from the fronts of World War I; others are setting off for the fronts of the great civil war. The famine of 1921 forces subsequent millions to roam in search of a piece of bread. Children whom the war and the Revolution have deprived of parents, those millions of miserable *bezprizorny* form hunger crusades that traverse the country in all directions. And later, throngs of labourers in search of work and bread travel to the Urals and other corners of the country, where they can find employment building factories, foundries, mines, dams. For more than forty years, tens of millions of people make the martyr's journey to the camps and prisons scattered over the entire territory of the superpower. The Second World War erupts, and subsequent multitudes are displaced in all directions, depending on where the front is. At the same time, behind these front lines, Beria directs the deportation of Poles and Greeks, Germans and Kalmuks, into the depths of the Caucasus and to Siberia. As a result, entire nations find themselves in lands foreign to them, in unfamiliar surroundings, in poverty and hunger. One of the goals of these operations is to create the uprooted man, wrenched from his culture, from his surroundings and land-scape, and therefore more defenceless and obedient vis à vis the dictates of the regime.[40]

The destruction of historic forms of common life was integral to the Soviet project. Forced-march industrialization dissolved communities more thoroughly than did the most extreme forms of capitalism in the West.

By the early thirties, the nobility and intelligentsia had mostly disappeared. Whatever survived of peasant life was killed off in the course of collectivization. The peasants became a defeated agricultural proletariat, while in the cities the Soviet regime created a drab replica of the Western bourgeoisie. Then, beginning in August 1936, the new communist elites were slaughtered in Stalin's purges. After the Great Terror came the Nazi invasion, with upwards of twenty-five million Soviet citizens dying resisting it. Following the end of the

Second World War, hundreds of thousands of Soviet soldiers who had been imprisoned in German camps were despatched to the Gulag, where many of them died.

Contrary to a popular Russian view, it was not Russia that suffered most from communism. The Mongolian People's Republic was a laboratory in the Soviet experiment in eradicating religion and collectivizing agriculture. Buddhist lamas were killed in massive numbers and nomadic herders deprived of their animals. By the spring of 1932, the population of Mongolia had fallen by a third.[41] Nothing on this scale happened in Soviet Russia, or in Mao's China. Only the death toll of the Cambodian regime of Pol Pot – variously estimated as being between 13 and 30 per cent of the population – comes close.

If Russians were not uniquely oppressed, neither were they altogether innocent. The genius of totalitarianism is that it make its victims complicit in its crimes. The Soviet novelist, social scientist and sometime émigré Alexander Zinoviev (1922–2006) went so far as to claim Stalin's rule was an expression of 'people power'. In *The Reality of Communism* (1986), he denied that Stalinism was a totalitarian system:

> The use of the term 'totalitarianism' in connection with Communist society hinders an understanding of that society. Totalitarianism is a system of coercion foisted upon a people 'from above' *independently of the social structure of the population*. The Communist system of coercion arose from the social structure itself, i.e. 'from below'.[42]

It would be truer to say that Soviet totalitarianism destroyed society and trapped the population in networks of mutual suspicion. This was the birthplace of *Homo Sovieticus* – not a new type of human being whose individual nature had merged into collective life, but a Hobbesian loner that survived by preying on others.

Zinoviev believed there was no way out from the Soviet system, but in 1989–91 a state that seemed everlasting evaporated almost overnight.[43] Western-inspired economic 'shock therapy' plunged much of society into poverty. Life expectancy dropped to levels common in emerging countries. Savings and careers built over decades became worthless in months or weeks. After an interlude under Boris Yeltsin's unsteady guidance Putin came to power, and consolidated his authority by moderating the chaos into which Russia had sunk. Then, beginning in March 2022, another way of life disappeared, as Putin closed down the relative freedom and prosperity that had prevailed under his authoritarian rule.

Unmaking one world to make another no less short-lived, apocalyptic events are normal in Russian history. Despite two world wars and many economic crises, wealth and freedom have increased in Western countries over the past hundred years. Against this background, the belief that history is a story of progress is a natural illusion.

If Russia's history does not show the gradual progress achieved in more fortunate Western states, neither does the model invoked by comparisons with fascism in interwar Europe. Once dictatorship was removed in these countries civil life re-emerged. The Russian state oversees a society immemorially habituated to tyranny. If despotic rule ends, it will probably be followed by a lengthy period of chaos and bloodshed.

That Russia is different from any European country has long been recognized. The French aristocrat the Marquis de Custine (1790–1857) described his impressions of the country in his *Letters from Russia*, published in 1843. A conservative who looked on the French Revolution with horror, Custine found in Russia a system so devoted to tyranny, and so wretched, that he believed it could survive only by conquering less despotic countries. 'The Russian people,' he wrote, 'have become unsuited for anything except the conquest of the world . . . Since I have been to Russia, I have taken a dark view of the future of Europe.'[44]

An earlier European traveller, the Savoyard diplomat and arch-reactionary Joseph de Maistre (1753–1821), despatched to Russia in 1802 as ambassador to the Russian imperial court for the kingdom of Piedmont-Sardinia, lived in Petersburg for fifteen years. Like Custine, though for different reasons, de Maistre was disappointed by Russia. He went there hoping to find a country that had not been touched by Enlightenment rationalism, only to find the Russian elites captivated by the French *philosophes*.[45] Without being a European country, Russia was infatuated with fashionable European ideas – a dangerous combination. Oscillating between passionate rejection of European modernity and delirious enthusiasm for rebuilding itself on a European model, Russia has never known liberty or the rule of law for any extended period.

Perhaps things could have been different. If the reforming Tsar Alexander II had not been assassinated in 1881 and the conservative modernizer Pyotr Stolypin in 1911; if the last tsar had not been so foolish, and the Menshevik leader, Alexander Kerensky, so weak; if Germany had not used Lenin to subvert the Russian war effort, or the Western Allies had not induced Russia to continue it; if post-communist Russia had not been pressured by the West to adopt a socially disruptive programme of economic shock therapy – if any of these contingencies had been otherwise, Russia might not have been ruled by despots for so long. As it is, there is little prospect of the country breaking with its tyrannical past.

Yet Russia is far from being what its Orthodox guardians would like it to be. In its ethical life it is like the West, only more so. Family breakdown, drug addiction, suicide and anomie run at higher levels than in most Western countries. The military, the intelligence services and the economy are rotted through with corruption. If Russia is a quasi-theocracy, it is also a full-blown kleptocracy. Common on the European far right and among American conservative culture-warriors, the idea that Russia is ethically superior to the West is a decadent fever-dream.

Putin's Leviathan is a ramshackle affair. Its armed forces recruit disproportionately from minority peoples, which bear the brunt of casualties in wars and are poorer than the Russian population. Less than half the population is Orthodox, with many practising other varieties of Christianity or else Islam, Buddhism or shamanism. (The Federation includes the Republic of Kalmykia, where a Tibetan-style variant of Buddhism is recognized as the majority religion.) Large numbers profess no faith at all. The Chechen Republic, headed by the warlord Ramzan Kadyrov, has operated as a semi-autonomous Islamic state since Putin appointed Kadyrov president in 2007, and some dissident Chechen forces are fighting on the Ukrainian side. There is no Russian world.

When Russia splintered a century ago, the Muslim regions and Siberia were the first to break away. The fall of the Soviet Union produced another breakup, with Ukraine, the Baltic states and the central Asian republics gaining independence. The invasion of Ukraine could be the trigger for a greater collapse: the final implosion of the Russian empire.

Western liberals may cheer,[46] but the process would not be peaceful. Almost inevitably it would involve bloodshed similar to that in former Yugoslavia, but on a much larger scale. With much of the country's natural wealth located in regions without Russian majorities, savage ethnic resource wars would be waged in which an authoritarian Muscovite regime struggled to suppress insurgent and conflicting nationalities. At the heart of these struggles would be one of the largest nuclear weapons arsenals in the world. A breakdown of Russian despotism comes with its own possibilities of apocalypse.

The Chinese Panopticon

It is in the laws of a commonwealth, as in the laws of gaming: whatsoever the gamesters all agree on, is injustice to none of them . . .

For the use of laws . . . is not to bind the people from all voluntary actions; but to direct and keep them in such a motion, as not to hurt themselves by their own impetuous desires, rashness or indiscretion; as hedges are set, not to stop travellers, but to keep them in their way . . . A law may be conceived to be good, when it is for the benefit of the sovereign, though it be not necessary for the people; but it is not so. For the good of the sovereign and people, cannot be separated. It is a weak sovereign, that has weak subjects; and a weak people, whose sovereign wanteth power to rule them at his will.

Leviathan, Chapter 30

Like Putin's Russia, Xi Jinping's China claims to be a state embodying a civilization apart from the West. The reality is more complicated. Xi's regime is supposedly based on Confucian values of social harmony. Yet he pays tribute to Mao Zedong, who between 1949 and the mid-1970s laid waste to Chinese civilization in the pursuit of an ugly occidental utopia. The totalitarian regime Mao imposed was a vehicle for a

Westernizing project transmitted from the Soviet Union. In Xi's China, however, Western ideologies other than Marxism-Leninism are in play.

Xi's project of nation-building originates in the illiberal West. The Chinese leader is not alone in this regard. The Hindutva ideology invoked by the Indian Prime Minister, Narendra Modi, is informed by Western ideas in which religion designates an exclusive identity, whereas indigenous Indian traditions are complex and many-sided. Islamist movements are also indebted to Western ideologies, notably Bolshevism and fascism, for some of their central themes.[47]

Some Western analysts have suggested that Xi's life experience led him to a Hobbesian idea of the state. Born in Beijing in 1953 into the Communist Party elite, he witnessed his father losing out in intra-party struggles and being humiliated and isolated. When the Cultural Revolution erupted in 1966, Red Guards surrounded Xi's school and some threatened to kill him. His half-sister perished from persecution. When, at the age of fifteen, Xi was sent to labour in a remote village, his banishment probably saved his life. In a rare personal interview in 2004, he stated that if he had stayed in the capital he was unsure 'if I would live or die'. An American analyst commented: 'A lot of people who came out of his experience in the Cultural Revolution concluded that China needed constitutionalism and the rule of law, but Xi Jinping said no: You need the Leviathan.'[48]

Suppressing the chaotic violence of the Cultural Revolution was a Hobbesian enterprise, but the state Xi built is not a Hobbesian Leviathan. Xi's attempt to unify the Chinese people in a single national culture echoes the interwar German jurist Carl Schmitt (1888–1985) more than Hobbes, while his system of government by surveillance is prefigured in the Panopticon, an ideal prison designed by the nineteenth-century British

Utilitarian philosopher Jeremy Bentham (1748–1832). Grafted onto a Marxist-Leninist stem, these illiberal Western ideologies underpin Xi's regime.

The continuing power of illiberal Western ideas is a neglected feature of the contemporary scene. China's intelligentsia has a grasp of Western thought exceeding that of many in Western universities. The study of Western classics is actively promoted in Chinese universities, where they are often taught in their original languages. Modern Western thinkers are also closely studied, including Hobbes and Leo Strauss, but Schmitt is seen by many Chinese intellectuals as having most to teach.

Schmitt gained academic recognition by showing the influence of theological ideas on jurisprudence. Later he promoted a theory of law as being created by the decisions of the sovereign that informed the Enabling Act of March 1933, which formally established the Nazi regime. In 1932 he published *The Concept of the Political*, arguing that law was made by the decisions of the sovereign, while politics was a struggle between enemies – in other words, a type of warfare.

Joining the Nazi party weeks after it came to power, Schmitt endorsed burning books by Jewish authors and proposed that scientific papers authored by Jews be marked with an identifying symbol. Despite these efforts to ingratiate himself, he was not fully accepted into the Nazi fold. In 1936 he was accused of opportunism and forced to resign from the party. At the end of the war he was arrested by Allied forces and spent a year in internment. He never recanted from his theories, elaborating on them until he was in his nineties.

Schmitt's theory in which law is made by the sovereign resembles that of Hobbes. The difference between the two thinkers is in their accounts of the purposes of the state. Whereas for Hobbes it was the protection of individuals from violence and insecurity – an essentially liberal view – Schmitt tasked the state with the protection of a unified people. It is this aspect of Schmitt's work that seems to attract Schmitt's disciples in China. If the state and the people are one and the same, minorities such as the Tibetans and the Uighurs can be suppressed, or obliterated, in the name of public safety.

The ideas of the German jurist have proved well suited to legitimating Xi's repression. In 2020 the Beijing law professor Chen Duanhong invoked Schmitt in a speech in Hong Kong supporting the National Security law, arguing that exercising China's sovereign authority to extinguish liberal freedoms in the former British colony was no more than the state securing its own future. Schmitt provides a template for Xi's project of nation-building.

The construction of nation-states had a European point of origin in revolutionary France. In the early 1790s, the Jacobins deployed an idea of the nation to crush a popular rising in the Vendée region of western France in a campaign of repression that cost in excess of 100,000 lives. The French nation-state continued to be built in the nineteenth century through military conscription and a single system of schooling. The cultural diversity that existed under the *ancien régime* was extinguished.

Ethnic cleansing became a central element in European nation-building in the aftermath of the First World War. The disintegration of the Habsburg, Romanov and Ottoman empires empowered demands for national self-determination, which were reinforced by the American president, Woodrow Wilson, in the Versailles peace settlement in 1919. Wilson aimed to rebuild the continent as a community of civic nation-states. He seems not to have fully understood that there were internal minorities in nearly all of these states. Huge numbers were expelled or fled – a million and a half Greeks from Turkey and around 400,000 Turks from Greece, for example.

During the Second World War, ethnic cleansing escalated into genocide. The Nazis killed millions in the territories they occupied in East Europe and the Soviet Union and attempted the complete extermination of Jews. Stalin deported peoples whose loyalty to the Soviet state he doubted (such as the Chechens and the Crimean Tartars) to remote regions in Central Asia, many of them dying on the journey or not long after their arrival.

Nation-states were constructed in nineteenth- and twentieth-century Europe, but polities where the majority of the citizens share the same ethnicity and culture may be much older. Something akin to nation-states emerged from population movements in early medieval Europe in the kingdoms of the Franks, Lombards and Danes. Nomadic peoples arriving from the east were among the first to create states defined by common cultures. An anthropologist's account of the role of the Eurasian steppe in the formation of modern Europe has suggested that 'the incipient idea of a nation-state might have been stronger with the nomadic groups from the steppe, who were bound more closely by tribal loyalties.'[49]

In China, nationalism developed towards the end of the Qing dynasty (1636–1912) as a reaction against the subjugation of the country by Western powers. Xi has sought to confer 'Chinese characteristics' on nation-building by citing Han Feizi, a third-century BC Han aristocrat and proponent of the Legalist School, which used law to build a more centralized Chinese empire. No doubt there are affinities, but Xi has built a state more homogeneous than any of China's empires. Over time it may become less monolithic. As Xi ages, there will be succession struggles. As often before in China's history, central authority may break up into warring states. Or the Westernizing project of a monocultural Chinese nation-state may be abandoned, and something more like a traditional empire return.

The model for Xi's project of total control is not Chinese but British. If anyone can be said to have originated the project of a surveillance society, it was Jeremy Bentham. The Panopticon was not only an ideal prison designed to keep inmates under observation at all times. It was intended for many other institutions – factories, workhouses, schools, hospitals and asylums – in fact, all of society. In prisons it would involve behaviour modification, with inmates segregated from one another, rewarded for obedience with food and straw for their cells and punished by hard rations and gagging. Prisoners would live in the perpetual glare of lamps installed at strategic points throughout the penitentiary.

Bentham's ideal prison resembles Xi's state in several ways. Today, cameras equipped with face-recognition technology monitor the population in their daily activities. Deviations from prescribed conduct are punished via China's social credit system. Databases managed by the National Development and Reform Commission, the People's Bank of China and the court system collect and assess reports of behaviour and on the basis of their findings give individuals a credit score. A negative rating can mean being banned from trains and planes, a positive score ensures priority health care and access to housing.

Xi imposed these technologies of control on a society that was already semi-demolished. Mao's legacy was a country in which pre-existing social structures had been systematically pulverized. The damage inflicted by the Cultural Revolution was not done only to buildings. Hundreds of millions of people were traumatized, first in the upheaval itself and then in its long aftermath. A scholar of Chinese classical art and literature who wrote under the name of Simon Leys summarized this experience:

> A skill the Chinese developed to the utmost proved to be their curse – the art of survival . . .
>
> . . . The 'Cultural Revolution' was a civil war that was prevented from running its full course. It is currently estimated by the Chinese themselves that nearly a *hundred million* people were to some extent directly involved in the violence of the 'Cultural Revolution' – either as active participants or as victims. More than ninety percent of the people who committed crimes during that period – murder, torture, looting – remain unpunished. The problem is not that they were not identified; on the contrary, it is simply that there are too many of them. In most cases, they were quietly reinstalled in their former positions. Since the bitterest fighting and the worst atrocities generally took place between rival factions within the walls of particular 'units' (administrations, factories, schools, etc.), now it is not rare to find murderers sharing the same office or the same cramped living quarters with the close relatives, associates, and friends of their victims. People who have been beaten up, denounced, betrayed, and sent to jail by their own colleagues or subordinates have to work again with them, side by side, day after day, as if nothing had ever happened between them.[50]

As in Stalin's Russia, the supreme achievement of Mao's regime was to implicate the people in its crimes. No one could escape the violence of the Cultural Revolution. Perpetrators became victims, and victims became perpetrators.

Since it has prevented any recurrence of violence of this

kind, Xi's regime may look like a Hobbesian state, but Hobbes's Leviathan had no interest in the curing of souls. China's system of labour camps, the *laogai*, has often been compared with the Gulag, and there can be little doubt that the Chinese system was constructed on a Soviet model, but memoirs of survivors show 'thought reform' was more central in China's camps. The purpose was to compel inmates to internalize the values of the Chinese state.[51]

Xi's Leviathan promotes a similar project in society at large. One of Xi's closest advisers, the political theorist Wang Huning, has argued that the Chinese state must inject a definite set of values into the population. Otherwise the country will undergo the decomposition that is underway in the US.

In August 1988, then a professor at Fudan University, Wang was invited to the US by the American Political Science Association. He reported his impressions and reflections during his six-month visit in a book, *America Against America* (1991). American society was in a process of deliquescence. The liberal individual is the product of values and practices that liberal societies undermine or destroy. Unchecked individualism becomes nihilistic subjectivity:

> Nihilism has become the American way, which is a fatal shock to cultural development and the American spirit, and as a result of this development, the American value system is declining and the entire democratic system is taking a huge hit . . .
>
> If society is left to develop naturally, traditional values will be difficult to preserve, and the trend of social development will always be to constantly eliminate the past . . . If it is democratic and people choose . . . the result of the choice is often self-explanatory. Who, then, will perform this social function?[52]

Wang's answer is the Chinese Communist Party. Led by a sovereign like Xi Jinping, the party will avert the slide into moral anarchy that has paralysed the US.

What is under way in China is not simply a reversion to dictatorship but a vast political experiment: the project of surpassing the scientific and technological advances of liberal societies while preserving social cohesion by means of an intelligent despotism. Wang was one of the few members of the Chinese Communist Party's Politburo Standing Committee to keep his position at the 20th Party Congress in Beijing in October 2022, where Xi became president for life.

Assisted by Western decay and disorder, Xi's project may yet succeed. Under the aegis of a hyper-Hobbesian ruler, China is using illiberal Western ideas to bury the remains of the liberal West.

The passing of the Anthropocene

And when all the world is overcharged with inhabitants, then the last remedy of all is war; which provideth for every man, by victory, or death.

Leviathan, Chapter 30

During the short post-Cold War era of globalization, a 'rules-based' global liberal order seemed to be in place, which some believed would endure indefinitely. This supposed liberal order is now history. If there was ever such a system, it exists no longer. Its passing has exposed the realities it concealed.

The post-Cold War global settlement was an artifact of US military supremacy, which began to break down with American overreach in Iraq and Afghanistan. With the invasion of

Ukraine in early 2022, international relations entered a phase like that which existed before 1914. The ensuing conflict highlighted the flimsiness of the structures built after the Cold War. The European Union is not an emerging super-state but a crypto-state lacking any military capacity to defend itself. Once the American security guarantee is withdrawn, the EU will be seen for what it is: a geo-strategic vacuum. Whatever the eventual upshot in Ukraine, there is no prospect of returning to the status quo that existed before the invasion.

While the West has been chasing phantoms, Russia has been practising a new kind of hybrid warfare. Putin blocked agricultural exports from the port of Odesa, a vital link with one of the world's great breadbaskets.[53] Facing defeat on the battlefield, he mounted a bombing campaign against Ukrainian infrastructure aiming to deny the civilian population electricity and water, all the while threatening nuclear escalation. Environmental destruction has become a strategy in warfare.

Meanwhile the late-nineteenth-century and early-twentieth-century Great Game of imperial rivalry has been given a new twist. Millions of electric vehicles, wind farms and solar panels will need stupendous quantities of minerals. Storing electricity requires batteries, which contain lithium, nickel, cobalt and other materials, necessitating mining on a prodigious scale, powered by oil, gas and coal. Renewable energy is a fossil fuel derivative. The transition to renewable energy in which so much has been invested in the West is a chimera.

Fossil fuels account for around 80 per cent of the world's current energy mix. Phasing them out completely would ruin states that rely on them for revenues. Bankrupted by falling prices, Saudi Arabia, Iran and Russia would implode. The upshot would be anarchy, with contending ethnic and sectarian groups contending for whatever resources remained of marketable value.

Spiralling demand for raw materials is spilling over in schemes for deep-sea mining. The melting Arctic cap offers further opportunities. Russia is enlarging its military presence there, while China is pushing for large-scale mining investments in the region and will use the new shipping lanes that are opening up to project its naval power into the Atlantic. The cap will become another zone of geopolitical conflict, and one of the Earth's last redoubts will be pillaged and despoiled.

A further twist comes with technologies that have created virtual environments. On Meta and other platforms, cyberworlds have come into being, but they depend on physical structures that can be disabled by war, revolution and climate change. People who have no working internet connection or electricity, hiding in basements in bombed-out cities or stranded in floods and droughts, cannot migrate into cyberspace. Nor are cyber-realms themselves zones of peace and safety. War and crime are rife in them. Since their material infrastructures are energy-intensive, virtual realms offer no escape from conflict over control of natural resources. The metaverse is a projection of the human world, not a way out of it.

The resurgence of geopolitics has been accompanied by the return of the planet as a deciding force in human events. Climate change and pandemic diseases destroyed the far-flung nexus that the Romans had built over centuries.[54] The Mayans in Mesoamerica, the Akkadian empire in Mesopotamia and the Khmer empire in south-east Asia were wiped out by overpopulation, drought and resource wars.

The belief that humans can escape dependency on the natural world is a modern conceit. The Anthropocene is not the age of human dominion but the moment when the position of the species on the planet comes into question. Here human numbers are crucial.

The canonical argument on overpopulation was presented by Thomas Malthus (1766–1834) in his *Essay on the Principle of Population*, where he argued that increasing human numbers exceed any increase in food production until they are rebalanced by famine, war and pestilence. In assuming that food production could not be increased, Malthus was mistaken. New agricultural technologies have fed much larger populations than he thought possible. In 1798, when he first published his essay, there were around 800 million human beings. By 2022 there were 8 billion. Not only had the population surged tenfold; large parts of it enjoyed living standards higher than most had done throughout history.

Nonetheless, in a roundabout manner he could not have foreseen, Malthus may yet be proven right. The rise in population was a by-product of hydrocarbons. Mechanized agriculture, pesticides, herbicides, fertilizers, refrigerators and battery farms require huge inputs of fossil fuels. Intensive farming is the extraction of food from oil. It is also part of the worldwide industrialization that has destabilized the climate. With the interacting crises in energy supply, climate change, pandemic diseases and chronic warfare, a brutal rebalancing of the kind Malthus foresaw may now be under way.

If so, it would not be unprecedented in modern times. A global crisis occurred in the mid seventeenth century, when a confluence of climate change, disease and war during the Little Ice Age reduced the human population of the planet by around a third. Those that remained lived in much reduced circumstances. The American historian Geoffrey Parker, author of a path-breaking study of the subject, comments that 'those who survived literally embodied Thomas Hobbes's assertion that: "the life of man" had indeed become "solitary, poor, nasty, brutish and short." '[55] Summarizing the military and political conflicts of the period, he writes:

> The 17th century saw a proliferation of wars, civil wars and rebellions and more cases of state breakdown around the globe than any previous or subsequent age. Just in the year 1648, rebellions paralyzed both Russia (the largest state in the world) and France (the most populous in Europe); civil wars broke out in Ukraine, England and Scotland; and irate subjects in Istanbul (Europe's largest city) strangled Sultan Ibrahim . . .
>
> Few areas of the world survived the 17th century unscathed by extreme weather. In China, a combination of droughts and disastrous harvests, coupled with rising tax demands and cutbacks in government programs, unleashed a wave of banditry and chaos . . . North America and West Africa both experienced famines and savage wars. In India, drought followed by floods killed over a million people in Gujarat between 1627 and 1630. In Japan, mass rebellion broke out on the island of Kyushu following several poor harvests. Five years later, famine, followed by an unusually severe winter, killed perhaps 500,000 Japanese.[56]

At the start of the twenty-first century, population growth is declining and reversing in many parts of the world, but still rising rapidly in some countries. Human numbers are projected to reach around 10 billion during the second half of the century, and only then fall globally. (The forecast assumes no large die-offs in the meantime.) Ten billion humans could be fed, but such an overpopulated world would be desperately fragile. The biosphere would be gutted by farming, wilderness would vanish and the planet would be increasingly unable to absorb greenhouse gases. As climate change advanced, there would be a growing temptation to experiment with geo-engineering.

Grandiose schemes have been mooted for injecting aerosols into the stratosphere, blocking off solar radiation and creating a planetary cooling effect. Cloud seeding – the dispersion of particles into the atmosphere with the aim of controlling rain and snowfall – is practised routinely in China. In December 2020 the State Council announced a programme of 'weather modification' over an area the size of India.

The risks of geo-engineering are clear. The planet would function like a patient being kept alive on a dialysis machine. There would be a built-in risk of system failure. Any malfunction could spell the end of the experiment.

Another danger is less often noted. Climate engineering will be deployed as a strategy in warfare. Cloud seeding was used by the Americans in Vietnam in Operation Popeye (1967–72) with the goal of disrupting North Vietnamese troop movements by extending the monsoon season. An international treaty was ratified by the UN in 1978 prohibiting military manipulation of the climate, but, as great-power rivalry continues, weather will surely become a weapon again.

High technology is the only way of achieving balance between the human animal and the planet. In a Promethean view, technology is an instrument of human dominion. In a humbler view, it enables what James Lovelock (1919–2022), the author of the Gaia theory in which life on Earth functions in some respects as a single organism, described as a sustainable retreat from planetary dominance.[57] The human footprint could be reduced by new modes of food production such as vertical farms, GM crops and lab-grown meat. Fossil fuels could be replaced by hydrogen power, modular nuclear reactors and nuclear fusion. The biosphere could be partially restored, and much of it rewilded.

The Earth treats human regimes with impartial indifference. It does not care whether they are capitalist or socialist, authoritarian or liberal. Only their material impact matters. Societies that treat climate change as a morality tale in which they are the villains will disappear, or be absorbed by others that are more pragmatic and resilient. Those that survive will understand that climate change is a shift that humans have caused but are unable to arrest. The only practical response is to adjust to it. Conceivably, global warming may occur at a rate that makes adaptation impossible. While the Earth functions as a system, there is no comparable coordination in the human world. In that case the planet will impose the necessary adjustment, regardless of humankind, and rewild itself.

One possibility is that global warming might be halted by a digital Leviathan. In 1997 the American historian of science George Dyson envisioned 'the convergence of biology and technology', which he argued was prefigured in the thought of Hobbes. 'By reason,' Hobbes wrote in the first chapter of *De Corpore* (1655), 'I understand computation.' Dyson goes on: 'We live in an age of embodied logic whose beginnings go back to Thomas Hobbes as surely as it remains our destiny to see new Leviathans unfold.' New kinds of artificial intelligence signal 'an end to the illusion of technology as human beings exercising control over nature, rather than the other way round'.[58] Lovelock, writing in 2019, foresaw cyborgs taking over the task of cooling the planet. 'We are now preparing to hand the gift of knowing on to new forms of intelligent beings.'[59]

However it may occur, the Anthropocene is coming to an end. Humankind is ceasing to be central in the life of the planet, so that life itself may go on.

2.

Artificial states of nature

Nature (the art whereby God hath made and governs the world) is by the *art* of man, as in many other things, so in this also imitated, that it can make an artificial animal. For seeing life is but a motion of limbs, the beginning whereof is in some principal a part within; why may we not say that all *automata* (engines that move themselves by springs and wheels as doth a watch) have an artificial life?

Leviathan, Introduction

Hobbes thought of Leviathan as an 'artificial animal' that human beings create to escape the state of nature. He did not anticipate that, through their attempts to remodel humanity, totalitarian regimes would create artificial states of nature.

Hobbes's lone individual is real enough. Emerging from a dream-filled womb, each human being acquires a social self by commingling with the dreams of others. The stranger within makes its appearance in extreme situations. At its height, the Soviet system was a state of chronic extremity. Living in constant fear of denunciation, people could not trust their family members, workmates, friends or lovers. The experiment in communism produced *Homo Sovieticus*, a species of Hobbesian solitaries.

Another experiment is underway in Western states captured by a hyperbolic version of liberalism. The hyper-liberal project is to emancipate human beings from identities that have been inherited from the past. Human beings must be free to make of themselves whatever they wish. The result is an artificial state of nature among self-defined identities.

Parallels between late nineteenth- and early twentieth-century Russia and the early twenty-first-century West may seem far-fetched. Their histories are very different. Never attempting to reconcile Athens and Jerusalem, Orthodoxy followed a different path from Western Christianity. There was no Reformation and no Renaissance. The Enlightenment had a profound impact, but was most influential in its least liberal forms. Liberalism did not die in Russia. It was never born.

Yet the similarities are real. Late tsarism and the late liberal West produced an intelligentsia that attacked the society that nurtured them. Both were under attack from within.

Portrait of an anti-liberal

. . . to please and delight ourselves, and others, by playing with our words, for pleasure or ornament, innocently.

Leviathan, Chapter 4

Even in his lifetime, Konstantin Leontiev (1831–91) was a neglected figure. The son of an officer who had been dishonourably discharged, he entered a military academy, then a medical school, and served as a doctor in the Crimean War. A peripatetic existence followed in which he was a journalist, editor and novelist, a minor Russian consular official in Crete and Ithaca, and a censor in the service of the tsarist state.

A sensualist who enjoyed sexual encounters with men and women, he married a Crimean girl, the daughter of a Greek merchant, who was unhappy with his extramarital activities and became mentally ill. Often unwell himself and nearly always in debt, he died in an Orthodox monastery, little known outside a small circle, and returned from oblivion only after the end of the communist era.

Leontiev was unusual in his thought as in his life. A thorough-going anti-liberal, he rejected nationalism and racial politics. He believed liberalism would evolve into a version of feudalism; but it was a prospect he welcomed. He proposed that the tsarist system should impose an autocratic socialism, which would be the new feudalism of which he dreamt. He was serious in these beliefs, but perhaps not entirely. He played with ideas as he did with his lovers, in order to contemplate their beauty.

This once forgotten thinker shows how conflicts between liberalism and its enemies are more complex than the antinomies of twenty-first-century debates. Opponents of liberal values are stereotyped as fascists; but Leontiev would have viewed twentieth-century fascism with distaste and horror, as he did nationalism in his own time, as a modern movement that destroyed the variegated order achieved in older societies. Leontiev's idea of a new Russian feudalism was chimerical, though no more so than the belief that Russia could become a communist utopia. In his analysis of the decline of the West he anticipated the German Oswald Spengler (1880–1936), though they were both premature in announcing it.

Among those who regard Leontiev as a thinker pertinent to the contemporary world has been Vladimir Putin. In a speech in September 2013, Putin stated: 'Russia – as the philosopher Konstantin Leontiev vividly put it – has always "blossomed in complexity" as a state-civilization, reinforced by the Russian people, Russian language, Russian culture, the Russian Orthodox Church and the country's other traditional religions.'[1]

Yet Leontiev was neither a Russian nationalist nor a Slavophile populist. He rejected ethnic nationalism as 'one of the strangest delusions of the nineteenth century'.[2] He was opposed to Russia trying to conquer and absorb related peoples: 'Our ideal ought to be, not union, but gravitational pull.'[3]

Leontiev's reputation as a reactionary comes from his years working with Konstantin Petrovich Pobedonostsev (1827–1907), Procurator of the Holy Synod under Tsar Alexander III, who reversed the liberal reforms of Alexander II after the latter's assassination in 1881. Though he failed to condemn the cruelly repressive measures the tsar imposed on the empire's Jewish population, Leontiev distanced himself from Pobedonostsev, describing him in a letter as 'not only not an originator, he's not even a reactionary, not a saviour, not a restorer, just a conservative in the narrowest sense of the word'.[4] Yet Leontiev had no time for the notion that Russia had a redemptive historical mission. As Berdyaev wrote, 'Leontiev was never given to mystical Messianism.'[5]

Russia's unique qualities originated in Byzantium, 'the strongest antithesis to the idea of all-mankind in the sense of earthly equality, earthly libertarian freedom, earthly total perfection and contentment'.[6] There was nothing especially Russian or Christian in Byzantine civilization. In the last year of his life, Leontiev wrote in a letter that a new Byzantinism should include Turkey, Iran, Syria, Palestine, Arabia, Egypt and Tibet.

Leontiev was Orthodox more than he was Christian. In July 1871, suffering from what he believed to be cholera while serving as Russian consul in Salonika, he was cured after praying to the Virgin Mary and promised he would take up monastic life.

His illness turned out to be malaria, and in two hours he was back on his feet. Three days later he was on Mount Athos. He reported the episode in a letter to his friend the writer Vasily Rozanov:

> I was seized by such horror at the thought of my physical demise that I suddenly found myself, in an instant, believing in the reality and power of the very Mother of God. I believed in her as strongly and intensely as if there was before me an actual living woman, a woman well known to me, kindly and all-powerful, and I cried out to her: 'Mother of God, I'm not ready to die yet, I've still done nothing worthy of my capabilities and I have led in the highest degree a life of dissolution and refined sinfulness. Raise me from this bed of death!'[7]

Saved by a miracle, as he believed, Leontiev returned to Salonika, where he burnt the manuscripts for a series of novels he had been writing, gave up his consular duties and went back to Athos. His life had taken a radical turn, though the ambiguities that preceded his mystical experience would never be fully resolved.

Leontiev describes his epiphany using the imagery of theism, and he lived afterwards in fear of divine punishment. But it was not so much God he revered as the Church. He turned to life as a monk in the hope that the prospect of unearthly beauty would liberate him from the pursuit of beauty through the senses. His goal was what he called 'transcendental egoism' – his own salvation.

For Leontiev, life had meaning only as an aesthetic experience. Beauty was worth more than truth or goodness – more, even, than civilization. In a short story, 'Chrizo', of 1868, he wrote of the Ottoman conquest of Greece: 'The Turks are barbaric, no question, but thanks to their bloody yoke the air of Cretan life is filled with the highest lyricism.'[8] Such assertions led him to him being dubbed 'the Russian Nietzsche'. But whereas the German pastor's son believed meaning could be created by an act of will, Leontiev looked for meaning in an act of surrender.

He dismissed any idea of Utopia because it meant deathly harmony. Civilizations and religions rose and fell in cycles. Some were better than others: Roman Catholicism and Islam were superior to Protestantism, medieval Europe to modern Europe. Leontiev was not a cultural relativist. Bourgeois civilization was one of the worst forms of life humankind had produced:

> . . . would it not be horrible and downright injurious to think that Moses ascended Mount Sinai, that the Hellenes built their graceful acropolises, the Romans waged their Punic wars, Alexander, that handsome genius, crossed the Granicus in a plumed helmet and fought at Arbela, that the prophets preached, the martyrs agonized, the poets sang, the artists painted and knights gleamed in tournaments – *only in order that the French, German, or Russian bourgeois in his ugly and comic* clothes should thrive 'individually and collectively' on the ruins of all this magnificent past?
>
> One would have to be ashamed of mankind if this vulgar ideal of universal utility, mean labor, and disgraceful prose should triumph forever!

Leontiev's hatred of bourgeois life meant insulating Byzantine civilization from Western influence: '. . . it is necessary to *freeze* Russia, if only slightly, in order to prevent it from "rotting." '[9] His vision of a tsarist socialism was a fantastical dream, but it confirmed that Leontiev had no attachment to the existing social order and was far from being a simple-minded reactionary.[10]

Leontiev's thought is so little known, and the circumstances in which it was produced so far from our own, that it may seem not much more than a historical curiosity. In some respects, though, he was strikingly perceptive. When he feared that a cult of individualism would threaten cultural diversity, he identified a pathology of liberal civilization.

Diversity is richest when societies are divided into distinct classes, with workers and peasants living differently from landowners and the bourgeoisie. As traditions are eroded, society is homogenized. Freedom in lifestyle means obedience to fashion. 'The tail-coat,' Lenontiev observed, 'is the mourning dress the West has adopted out of grief for her magnificent, religious, aristocratic and artistic past.'[11]

Leontiev was not referring only to outward signs of conformity such as dress. The inner lives of supposedly autonomous individuals, their hopes and dreams, are remarkably alike. Universal individualism and mass society are not opposites but different sides of the same form of life. This fact was noted by Alexis de Tocqueville and John Stuart Mill, liberals who feared individualism would result in majority tyranny. Neither of them came up with any way of preventing the outcome they dreaded.

When speculating about the future, Leontiev found himself in unexpected company. The Victorian laissez-faire liberal Herbert Spencer argued that socialism required authoritarian rule. Leontiev agreed:

Socialism is ever more clearly, in theory and practice, revealing its despotic character. As I write, the liberal Spencer is disseminating his book against socialism – The Coming Slavery. He prophecies that socialism can only be realized on the basis of slavish subordination to the collective and to government. And I believe he is right.

Unlike Spencer, Leontiev welcomed the coming despotism. He compared the socialist sects of his day to early Christian communities. In a letter of March 1889 he wrote:

> I am of the opinion that socialism in the twentieth and twenty-first centuries will start to play that role in the sphere of government and economics which Christianity used to play in the sphere of government and religion in the days when she began to triumph . . . Socialism is now in the stage of martyrdom, and its earliest congregations, scattered here and there, but it will find its Constantine . . . What is now the doctrine of revolution will then be the apparatus of repression, the instrument of extreme compulsion, discipline, perhaps even of slavery . . . Socialism is the feudalism of the future.[12]

Spencer and Leontiev were both mistaken in their predictions. There was no convergence on either liberalism or socialism. From Bismarck onwards, Western countries adopted varieties of collectivism without becoming socialist states. An autocratic type of socialism was imposed on Russia, but instead of preserving rural life it exterminated the peasantry. Communism was a highly stratified order, as Leontiev predicted. But it eliminated the aristocracy as well as the peasantry, while the communist elites were in turn destroyed in campaigns of terror. Russia became an impoverished version of the bourgeois world Leontiev despised.

He realized that his vision of modern feudalism was a mirage. 'Reaction is not a radical cure,' he wrote, 'but only a temporary reprieve for an organism that is *already* affected by an *incurable* disorder.'[13] Yet he could not have foreseen Russia as it became, under Putin, a mix of theocracy and kleptocracy.

It is fortunate that Leontiev did not believe happiness to be the goal of life, for he had little of it himself. He died believing he had 'tried his hand at everything and brought no benefit to anyone, apart from three or four people'.[14]

'A Cassandra, Leontiev, wandering through Troy and prophesying, and like her, no one listened to him.'[15] So wrote his follower Vasily Rozanov, three months before dying of starvation in 1919 in a monastery outside Moscow. Twenty-seven years earlier, Leontiev had died in the same monastery. The two writers are buried side by side in the cemetery of a nearby hermitage.

The curtain comes down

. . . things *to come* have no being at all, the future being but a fiction of the mind . . .

Leviathan, Chapter 3

In a fragment to which he gave the title 'La Divina Commedia', Vasily Rozanov wrote:

With a clanking, creaking and squeaking, an iron curtain is belong lowered on Russian history.

'The show is over.'

The audience rises.

'It's time to put on our coats and go home.'

They look around.

But there are no coats to put on, and no houses to go home to.[16]

Rozanov was notorious for his contradictory attitudes. He praised ancient-Egyptian religion while lauding the Russian Orthodox Church, and propagated the vilest anti-Semitic slanders while passionately admiring Judaism. Preaching the sanctity of family life, he also exalted sexuality, not only between men and women but in those who loved others of the same sex, 'lunar people', whom he credited with many of humankind's cultural achievements. Though he wrote mostly for a conservative newspaper in which he defended monarchy and the established order, for a time he published simultaneously under a pseudonym in a liberal journal, where he condemned the tsarist system in the strongest terms.

Rozanov's critics condemned him as an amoral opportunist, and it cannot be denied that at times he pandered to the worst forces of his time. He has been defended on the ground that he needed to earn money to support his family. It would be truer to say he found cynicism a more comfortable pose than hypocrisy. He lived as one who mocked all that was revered as holy, but died an Orthodox believer.

His attitude to Christianity was complex. Nietzsche praised Jesus while condemning the Church: 'in reality there has been only one Christian, and he died on the Cross.'[17] Rozanov welcomed the fact that the Church had ignored Jesus's message. 'Christ never planted a tree, never engendered the tiniest blade of grass . . . Fundamentally He is not a being but almost a phantom, a shade, which by some miracle passed over the earth. Shade, shadow, emptiness, nonbeing – such is His substance.'[18]

He hated the Christian redeemer with his bitter message that happiness comes only with the end of earthly things, and cherished the Orthodox Church for the ways in which it sweetened the small pleasures of life. (Rozanov loved jam.) Instead of preaching the end-time, the Church made the joys of daily life seem everlasting.

Rozanov was an anti-apocalyptic thinker whose fate was to live through an apocalypse. Originating in Jewish scripture, the idea of apocalypse combines two meanings, mystical and eschatological: a revelation and the end of a world. For Rozanov, the apocalyptic event was the Russian Revolution. A world ended, but nothing was revealed.

Born in 1856, the son of a forester and a mother who claimed descent from a noble family, he grew up in a small village in provincial Russia. His family was of modest means though not poor. He spent many years working as a schoolmaster, longing to live in St Petersburg. He venerated Dostoevsky, whose mercurial former lover Apollinaria Suslova he married and lived with for six unhappy years, and produced a book-length interpretation of Dostoevsky's legend of the Grand Inquisitor.[19] It appears to be Rozanov who coined the expression 'iron curtain', which Winston Churchill used in a famous speech in March 1946 to describe the division of the Soviet Union from the West at the start of the Cold War.

Rozanov cut an unprepossessing figure:

> In the nineties of the last [i.e. nineteenth] century there could sometimes be seen in St Petersburg newspaper offices a rather small, thin, nervous man with a heavy reddish moustache stained with tobacco and a short beard, who resembled in his general appearance a schoolmaster or a railway booking-office clerk. No one seeing him would guess that he was among the masters of Russian literature.[20]

He did not pretend to any system of ideas. His four main books – *Solitaria*, two volumes of *Fallen Leaves* and *The*

Apocalypse of Our Time – were 'baskets' of random thoughts, recorded in the course of cleaning his pipe, examining his coin collection and other daily activities. It was Rozanov's casual dismissal of weighty pieties that attracted D. H. Lawrence, who cited jottings such as 'I am not such a scoundrel yet as to think about morals' and 'Try to crucify the Sun, and you will see which is God.'[21]

Rozanov left the teaching profession when an article he wrote attacking the Russian education system incurred the disapproval of the authorities. A friend arranged for him to be given a minor bureaucratic post in St Petersburg, and he realized his dream of becoming a metropolitan author. But he was too idiosyncratic to fit into any literary circle. Even after his death, he was a suspect figure. In his book *Literature and Revolution* (1923), Leon Trotsky singled him out as 'a wormlike person and writer: wriggly, slippery, sticky, contracting and stretching to need – and like a worm, repellent.'[22]

In his youth, Rozanov read the works of Dimitri Pisarev (1840–68), one of the founders of the Russian nihilist movement. In nineteenth-century Russia, nihilism meant something different from – indeed, opposite to – what it means at present. A nihilist was not someone who believed in nothing but one who believed only in science. All the religions and moralities of the past were worthless, if not positively harmful, and had to be replaced by a strictly rational way of thinking. This kind of nihilism is illustrated in the character of Yevgeny Bazarov in Ivan Turgenev's novel *Fathers and Sons* (1862).

The Russian nihilists revered science with a fervour approaching idolatry. As Berdyaev wrote:

Nihilism is the negative of Russian apocalyptic. It is a revolt against the injustices of history, against false civilization; it is a demand that history shall come to an end, and a new life, out-side or above history, begin. Nihilism is a demand for nakedness, for the stripping from oneself of all historical traditions, for the setting free of the natural man, upon whom there will no longer be fetters of any sort.[23]

A vapid brand of nihilism can be found in the writings of rationalists such as Steven Pinker.[24] Of course, they would indignantly reject this description of their beliefs. Yet none of them has presented any justification for the liberal values they profess. Their belief in the liberating power of science is more contrary to reason than any traditional faith, for it ignores the well-attested fact that science can just as well serve oppression as freedom.

Rozanov's apocalypse came with the breakdown of the Russian *ancien régime*. 'Russia faded out in two days,' he wrote. 'At most three.'[25] It was also the end of his life. His livelihood disappeared when the newspaper for which he had been writing for eighteen years was closed down after the Bolsheviks took power. He continued to write, publishing *The Apocalypse of Our Time* as a series of roughly printed pamphlets, which he sold to subscribers, sometimes asking for payment in food or clothing, until illness made that too impossible. Having fled with his remaining valuables to a small town near a centuries-old monastery not far from Moscow, he had his coin collection stolen. With no income apart from what his daughters earned as housemaids, he picked up cigarette butts in the streets and begged for glasses of tea from shop-owners. In one of his last visits to Moscow, in the autumn of 1918, he was taken to the Soviet centre of power. On the way he stopped a passer-by in the street, demanding, 'Do show me, please, a real live Bolshevik. I should very much like to see one.' At the Soviet he said, 'Show me the head of the Bolsheviks – Lenin or Trotsky. I am Rozanov, the monarchist.'[26]

Rozanov's death went unnoticed. Before he died, partially paralysed, he asked that all he had written against Jews be destroyed. In 1911 he had published shameful pieces endorsing the prosecution of a Ukrainian Jew, Mendel Beilis, who had been accused of the ritual murder of a young Christian boy. In giving credence to the infamous blood libel, Rozanov reached his lowest point. On the brink of death, he seems to have repented.

Reconciling with the Orthodox Church, he spent his last days crying 'Christ is risen!' After receiving the last sacrament four times, at his request, he passed away on 5 February 1919. The mother of his children, with whom he had lived happily for three decades, survived him for four years. One of his daughters, who had become a nun, hanged herself not long after his death. His son died soon after from the Spanish flu. His three other daughters lived on, the last of them dying in 1975.

Rozanov's style of writing has few parallels. *The Book of Disquiet* by the Portuguese writer Fernando Pessoa (1888–1935) comes closest. Like Rozanov's most characteristic writings, it is composed from thoughts recorded on scraps of paper. But Pessoa's author is a fictional character, whereas Rozanov's scraps were thrown off by the man himself, who was struggling to produce something other than literature as it had hitherto been understood. The Russian cultural theorist Viktor Shlovsky wrote of *Solitaria* that it was 'a heroic effort to leave the bounds of literature, to express oneself without words, without form – and the book turned out splendidly, because it created a new type of literature, a new form'.[27]

In a passage entitled 'Pinned Down by a Bookcase', Rozanov wrote of humankind being crushed under the weight of books, producing 'a strange, groaning civilization'. It was necessary to push the bookcase aside, 'to start the whole business over again from the beginning'.[28] Elsewhere he wrote, 'I endure literature as my grave, I endure literature as my sorrow, I endure literature as my disgust.'[29] And, most decisively, 'There is no doubt that it was literature that killed Russia. Those elements that effectively devastated Russia all had literary origins.'[30]

Rozanov was sufficiently broad-minded to find some value in liberalism:

> There are certain conveniences in liberalism, without which 'one feels awkward'. Under liberalism there will be many schools, and I shall have somewhere to send my son. And in a liberal school they will not flog him, but will treat him gently and nicely. If I myself fall ill I shall call in an enlightened doctor, who will not confuse heart disease with appendicitis . . . Thus 'progress and 'liberalism' are a trunk 'made in England', in which you can 'put everything quite conveniently', and which even a nonliberal would prefer to take on his journey.[31]

He hated the Bolshevik revolution because it destroyed the familiar world. A generation of the intelligentsia found their life in Russia had come to a close. In September and October 1922, in a scheme devised by Lenin, over 200 of them were deported from Russia on a pair of steamships.[32] If they stayed, their safety was not guaranteed. Many Russian thinkers left, along with historians, linguists, musicians and cultural figures. Later, others exited the country by train. Somewhere between one and two million Russians – not only supporters of the Whites in the Civil War but anti-Bolshevik socialists and revolutionaries, social democrats and many of no political affiliation – joined the exodus from the Bolshevik regime.

Almost exactly a century after the steamships sailed, another generation of Russians was leaving after the invasion of Ukraine in February 2022. Vladimir Putin was shutting down the life of the mind as Lenin had done. The ideology he invoked was different, but the curtain was lowered again.

Rozanov saw the Russian Revolution as an absurdist comedy, and something not dissimilar is being staged in Western countries today. Liberalism has once again become a creature eating its own tail. The current generation of liberals never tires of denouncing the West as the most destructive force in history – racist, imperialist and sexist. Education must be 'de-colonized' in order to expose the West's unique crimes. Western civilization has been a curse for humankind.

Yet these same liberals insist that Western values – human rights, personal autonomy and the like – must be projected to the last corners of the Earth. The avowed goal is to liberate human beings from identities they have accidentally acquired. Stripped of these contingencies, they can be whatever they wish.

Words and demons

The universities have been to the nation, as the wooden horse was to the Trojans.

Thomas Hobbes, *Behemoth*, Dialogue 1

The decades that led up to revolution in tsarist Russia display several features that presage the twenty-first-century West. One is the rise of an antinomian intelligentsia, which professes to instruct society by deconstructing its institutions and values.

In the history of religion, antinomians assert that salvation can be achieved only by rejecting rules imposed by the Church and obeying the voice of the spirit. In late-medieval times, antinomian enthusiasm mobilized mass movements recruited from displaced peasants and the urban poor. These estranged populations aimed to overturn society in the faith that Christ was about to return in a thousand-year-long reign of peace and harmony.

There are parallels between medieval millenarian and modern revolutionary movements. Millenarians believed the new age would be ushered in by God, modern revolutionaries by 'humanity'.[33] The most long-lasting of the medieval movements was the Brotherhood of the Free Spirit. Extending across large parts of Europe for over three centuries, the Brethren considered themselves emancipated from the constraints of morality. Norman Cohn writes:

> They were in fact Gnostics intent upon their own individual salvation; but the gnosis at which they arrived was a quasi-mystical anarchism – an affirmation of freedom so reckless and unqualified that it amounted to a total denial of every kind of restraint and limitation. These people could be regarded as remote precursors of Bakunin and Nietzsche – or rather of that bohemian intelligentsia which during the last half-century has been living from their ideas in their wilder moments.[34]

Late-nineteenth-century Russian revolutionaries and early twenty-first-century Western hyper-liberals have much in common. In each case, a swollen lumpen-intelligentsia has become a powerful political force. Both hold to the faith that human beings possess powers that used to be ascribed to the Deity. Both – Russian radicals knowingly, twenty-first-century hyper-liberals unthinkingly – are engaged in a project of God-building.

A movement whose members described themselves as

God-builders appeared in the early twentieth century as a heterodox faction of the Bolsheviks and their sympathizers, including the Commissar of Enlightenment, Anatoly Lunacharsky (1875–1933),[35] and the novelist Maxim Gorky (1868–1936). They were inspired by the Orthodox philosopher Nikolai Federov (1829–1903), who believed technology would enable the physical resurrection of every human being that had ever lived, and, in Lunacharsky's case, by Nietzsche's idea of the *Übermensch*, a higher type of human that could be willed into being. The God-building movement was not encouraged by Lenin or Stalin, and by the 1930s no longer existed.[36]

A prescient critique of the ideas expressed in later God-building movements appears in the writings of Fyodor Dostoevsky (1821–81). The novelist's own outlook – a toxic brew of pan-Slavism, anti-Semitism and Russian messianic myths – is of no interest. His insights into the mindset of Russian terrorists and their intellectual fellow travellers are acutely relevant to twenty-first-century liberalism.

As Dostoevsky saw it, Russian atheism was a flight from a godless world. Rather than learning how to live without God, it aimed to build a new God through the divinization of the human species. Atheism has not always been a vehicle for this ambition.[37] Some atheists have rejected not only any notion of a creator-god but also the idea that human beings can create themselves or their world. The German philosopher Arthur Schopenhauer regarded human agency as an illusion. In literature the supreme exponent of this atheism is Samuel Beckett.

A lucid formulation of God-building appears in Dostoevsky's novel *Demons*, otherwise translated as *Devils* or *The Possessed*, first published in 1871. The protagonists play out a grim comedy. Stepan Trofimovich Verkhovensky is a failed academic who serves as the tutor of Nikolai Vsevolodovich Stavrogin, a charismatic but indolent son of a rich landowner, Varvara Petrovna Stavrogina, with whom Stepan has an ambiguous relationship and on whom he is financially dependent. Ivan Shatov, the son of a former serf who has turned his back on revolution and become an Orthodox believer, is killed by Stepan's disciples at his instigation. Alexei Nilych Kirillov is an engineer who kills himself in order to assert his divinity.

Verkhovensky represents a type of intellectual familiar the world over. Recycling the fashionable detritus that millions like him unthinkingly believe, he is convinced of his independence of mind. He denounces society while never doubting its stability or his place in it. Gleefully conniving in the destruction of traditional morality, he is pitifully unprepared for the savagery that ensues when it breaks down.

The action in the novel is based on an event that took place when Dostoevsky was writing the book. A revolutionary, Sergei Nechaev (1847–82), was arrested for complicity in the murder of a student who belonged in the terrorist group Nechaev headed. The murder of Shatov by Verkhovensky's terrorist disciples replicates this incident and shows the consequences of Nechaev's philosophy.

In *The Catechism of a Revolutionary*, a pamphlet published in 1869, Nechaev argued that any crime was justified if it helped bring about the victory of the revolution. All human beings were expendable. This included fellow revolutionaries, if killing them brought a new world nearer. As Albert Camus noted, 'Nechaev's originality thus lies in justifying the violence done to one's brothers.'[38] Many later revolutionaries were influenced by Nechaev's catechism, including Lenin, though he rejected his reliance on individual acts of terror.

Dostoevsky foresaw that Nechaev's pursuit of complete freedom would lead to absolute tyranny. A minor character in the novel, Shigalyov, confesses:

> Having devoted my energy to studying the question of the future society which is to replace the present one, I have come to the conclusion that all creators of social systems from ancient times to our year of 187— have been dreamers, tale tellers, fools who contradicted themselves and understood precisely nothing of natural science or that strange animal known as man . . . I got entangled in my own data, and my conclusion directly contradicts the original idea from which I start. Starting with unlimited freedom, I conclude with unlimited despotism. I will add, however, that apart from my solution of the social problem, there is no other.[39]

Unlimited freedom means turning oneself into a god. Kirillov explains:

> To recognize that there is no God, and not to recognize at the same time that you have become God, is an absurdity, otherwise you must necessarily kill yourself. Once you recognize it, you are king and you will not kill yourself but live in the chiefest glory. But one, the one who is first, must necessarily kill himself, otherwise who will begin and prove it? It is I who will necessarily kill myself in order to prove it . . . For three years I have been searching for the attribute of my divinity, and I have found it: the attribute of my divinity is – Self-will![40]

In Kirillov's atheism, God's powers are not transferred to 'humanity'. They are assumed by him, and him alone. A precedent for this kind of atheism can be found in the German philosopher Max Stirner (1806–56), who attacked secular humanist values as 'spooks' in *The Ego and Its Own*, published in 1844. (The book was translated and published in Russia, but it is not known whether Dostoevsky read it.) Progress and human rights, society and humankind itself are all of them ghosts, exercising a demonic power over human beings. But Stirner was himself possessed by spooks. He writes:

> God and mankind have concerned themselves for nothing, for nothing but themselves. Let me then likewise concern myself for myself, who am equally with God the nothing of all others, who am my all, who am the only one.
>   . . . I am the creative nothing, the nothing out which I myself as creator create everything.[41]

The unique one is not a frail human being but an avatar of the Deity. Atheism was the deification of the human subject. Here Stirner and Nietzsche, Nechaev and Bakunin, were at one.

A similar project is pursued in the hyper-liberal idea of self-creation. The result is a pastiche of worn-out ideas. The comedy of self-creation is highlighted in *The Brothers Karamazov*, when Ivan encounters the Devil during a bout of delirium:

> This was a person, or more accurately speaking a Russian gentleman of a particular kind, no longer young . . . He was wearing a brownish reefer jacket, rather shabby but evidently made by a good tailor though, and of a fashion at least three years old, that had been discarded by smart and well-to-do people for the last two years . . . there was every appearance of gentility on straitened means.

The Devil summons up the vision that bewitched the Russian intelligentsia:

> ... everything will begin anew. Men will unite to take from life all it can give, but only for joy and happiness in the present world. Man will be lifted up with a spirit of divine Titanic pride and the man-god will appear. From hour to hour extending his conquest of nature infinitely by his will and his science, man will feel such lofty joy from hour to hour in doing it that it will make up for all his old realms of heaven. Everyone will know that he is mortal and will accept his death proudly and serenely like a God ... since there is no God and no immortality, the new man may become the man-god, even if he is the only one in the world, and promoted to his new position, he may light-heartedly overstep all the barriers of the morality of the old slave-man, if necessary ... There is no law for God ... 'all things are lawful', and that's the end of it.[42]

The Devil aims not to emancipate humankind but to corrupt it with a deceptive idea of freedom. The demons of which Dostoevsky wrote were not terrorists. They were ideas, which wrought destruction on the society the intelligentsia aimed to liberate, and on the intelligentsia themselves.

Kirillov shoots himself after claiming responsibility for the murder of a student revolutionary accused of being a police informant. He is encouraged by the Byronic nobleman Stavrogin, who also ends by killing himself. In a chapter of the book entitled 'At Tikhon's', omitted by the publisher from the original edition, Stavrogin declares his disbelief in God and rejects any distinction between good and evil. He goes on to confess to having raped an eleven-year-old girl, then driving her to suicide. Later he seems to acknowledge complicity in the death of his disabled wife. Stavrogin is addicted to the excitement that comes with transgressing moral laws in whose existence he does not believe.

Verkhovensky dies half rejecting the revolutionary ideas he half-believed. Making a pilgrimage to a monastery, he becomes ill and is joined by Varvara Stavrogina. He undergoes a deathbed conversion to Orthodoxy, though the narrator expresses some doubt as to its genuineness. A poseur whose disguises mask an inner nullity, he is no more a rebel than Ivan's devil. He belongs in the class of 'the wise' satirized in Dostoevsky's short story 'The Dream of a Ridiculous Man':

> ... people appeared who began devising ways of bringing men together again, so that each individual, without ceasing to prize himself above all others, might not thwart any other, so that all might live together in harmony. Wars were waged for the sake of this notion. All the belligerents firmly believed at the same time that science, wisdom and the instinct for self-preservation would eventually compel men to unite in a rational and harmonious society, and therefore, to speed up the process in the mean time, 'the wise' strove with all expedition to destroy 'the unwise' and those who failed to grasp their idea, so that they might not hinder its triumph.[43]

Verkhovensky is playing with forces he does not begin to understand. By colluding in the destruction of freedoms that do exist, he helps create a tyranny more complete than any that existed before. Liberal intellectuals like him were among the first to be deported or liquidated in Lenin's Russia.

The history of communism vindicated Dostoevsky's prophecies. Tens of millions of human beings died in an attempt to create a new humanity. The communist experiment illustrates a Hobbesian truth on which all such projects founder. Human beings are material and perishable. In extreme situations, the words they use to make themselves into persons no longer work.

Dystrophy and coal-black bread

> . . . if in a great famine he takes food by force, or stealth, which he cannot take by money, nor charity . . . he is totally excused . . .
>
> *Leviathan*, Chapter 27

'At night, lying on a sofa next to a stove stocked with furniture and picture frames, Boldyrev read novels.'[44] A scholar in Persian literature at the Hermitage Museum in Leningrad, Alexander Boldyrev was an expert in survival. He avoided the purges that swept through the Soviet Union in the 1930s by spending time in hospital and making research trips to Central Asia, and evaded military conscription through the intervention of a lover at the Museum. Along with his wife and daughter, he outlived the 900-day siege of Leningrad, 1941–4, during which somewhere close to a million people died.

No one could survive on government food rations alone. Boldyrev bartered family heirlooms for food, selling watches, a cigarette holder, porcelain, cutlery and his mother's wedding ring for flour, fat and bread. He inveigled his way into institutions at whose canteens he ate and from which he could bring home edible scraps. His mother, brother-in-law and uncle perished from malnutrition. He hung on, and died in 1993.

A survivor recalled a co-worker at the literary institute Pushkin House:

> I remember the death of Yasinsky. He had once been a tall, slim, very handsome old man, who reminded me of Don Quixote. During the winter he moved to the Pushkin House library, sleeping in a folding bed, behind the book stacks . . . His mouth wouldn't close, and saliva trickled from it; his face was black, making an eerie contrast with his completely white, unkempt hair. His skin was taut over his bones . . . His lips became thinner and thinner and failed to cover his teeth, which protruded and made his head look like a tortoise's.[45]

Like others who sought sanctuary in Pushkin House, Yaskinsky was not allowed to die there. In order to avoid the chore of removing their corpses, dying members of staff were thrown out by the deputy director onto the street, where they would perish of cold. Their bodies lay unattended until they were stripped of their clothes and boots by passers-by. The streets were dangerous places. A sudden shriek could signal the theft of a ration card – a death sentence for the victim.

Families often cracked under the strain. Some worked together finding food, with mothers and fathers sacrificing nourishment so their offspring could live a little longer. In others there were reports of family members eating the bodies of their parents, children, spouses or other relatives after they had starved to death.

Sex was traded, not for money, now a secondary currency, but food. Among 'old, doomed people', 'cafeteria girls' stood out for their 'healthy blooming faces'. Men offered favours to female food service workers. Both were distinguished from the rest of the population by retaining physical signs of their sex, visible in bath houses, which marked them out from many in the city who had become virtually androgynous under the strain of hunger.[46]

Those who survived the blockade did so as different persons. As their bodies lived on, fed by their remaining flesh, they became strangers to themselves. Diaries record the shock they felt when they looked into a mirror. One woman wrote: 'I look like all those other devils, I have become just bones and wrinkled skin.' Addressing herself by the name of the person she had been, she continued: 'Compared to what you were during the first days of the war, you have become unrecognizable, Sasha.' Another, when she saw herself in a mirror, spat at her reflection.

A historian comments:

> The diarists were not only trapped inside the city; they were imprisoned in unfamiliar bodies produced by starvation . . . The mirror not only displayed surface-level changes to personal appearance; it alerted the diarists to more fundamental changes in their anatomy and psychology. Body parts and systems operated in new, unpredictable ways . . . The siege transformed them into qualitatively different human beings, into blokadniki.[47]

The words they used to describe themselves in the past may have lost much of their meaning, but these new human beings were not always without voice. Some of them produced verse, clandestinely written to avoid punishment by the authorities. Sometimes these poems were shown to no other human being. The art historian Gennady Gor (1907–81) left a yellowing notebook containing poems he never mentioned to anyone, which was found after his death by his grandson. In one of them, he reimagined the cannibalism practised during the siege:

> I ate Rebecca the girl full of laughter . . .
> A raven looked down but it was for nothing
> I didn't throw it the arm of Rebecca.[48]

Those who knew Gor in later life could not believe these savage verses had been written by the person they knew – 'a timid, sarcastic eccentric'.[49] When he returned to the shrouded everyday world, this poet of extremity became yet another person, whose previous selves were invisible to those he met and perhaps to himself.

It did not take long for the inhabitants of the city to be divided into those with access to food and those without. For those in the latter category, 'dystrophia' was registered as the cause of death.

For most of the population, access to food depended on their place of work. Defence factories were among the best, though the death rate from accidents was high and workers in bakeries had better prospects of surviving. The worst off were refugees from the countryside and inmates of institutions. Fleeing the advancing Germans, peasant families were turned back to be housed in empty buildings in the suburbs or camps at the edges of the city. After killing their animals for food, they starved and froze to death. Unknown numbers of children in orphanages and patients in hospitals died in the same way.

The closer you were to power, the less likely you were to die of dystrophy. Best off of all were those who worked at the party headquarters. An instructor in the cadres department recorded breakfast with macaroni or spaghetti, lunch with vegetable soup, sour cream and mince patty. Holidaying in a

Soviet 'rest house', he dined on chicken, goose, turkey, sausage and fish, accompanied by cocoa, tea, coffee, wine and port. Power and survival were twins.

Leningrad during the siege was an artificial state of nature in two respects. By cordoning off the city, the invading Nazi forces created a world of extreme scarcity sealed off from the rest of the Soviet Union. But from its beginnings, Soviet society was the site of a war for food.

The American left-wing journalist Eugene Lyons, who arrived in the Soviet Union in 1928, reported:

> Another sign of the renewed pressure on the *byvishiye* – 'former people' – was the sudden opulence of the 'commission shops.' These emporia, several on every main street, either bought goods outright from individuals and resold them for several times as much, or accepted articles for sale on a percentage basis. They now began to fill up with antiques, silver, furs, old furniture, rare ceramics, paintings, miniatures, jewelery, rugs . . .

Special hard-currency stores became cornucopias stacked with the supreme luxury – white bread:

> The miracle of white bread: crisp little loaves in a glowing heap . . . Not the sand-gray bread that passed, at double prices, for white in the ruble stores, but luminously real. At the other end of the long angular shop was the jewelery department. Its litter of rubies and diamonds for foreign buyers had not half the radiance of the white loaves; precious stones shine with a cold inner glitter, whereas white loaves are prisms to reflect fascination in the eyes of hungry Russians. There was butter, too, and cheeses, bland Volga salmon and great flanks of

blood-dripping meat. But the white bread outshone them all – at once substance and symbol of desire.[50]

The poet Polina Barskova, now living and working in the United States, recalls her parents, who lived through the siege, showing her

> . . . a piece of the black matter (made of something completely inedible) that was rationed in the city during the winter of 1941–2.
> And I still remember the taste of tears in my throat when I saw it: this bread looked like coal, like something from Hell.[51]

Life itself was rationed. Only those with connections could hope to live on, and not for long. Between 1937 and 1938, around 2 million people were arrested and around 700,000 executed. The Great Terror was extreme not only in the numbers of lives that were ended. It destroyed much of the new ruling class that emerged from the Bolshevik revolution. An account of the year would have to show the elite

> . . . at the moment when, following the breath-taking rise of so many careers, they all plunged once more into the abyss. It would be a story of rise and fall in a historical second; it would portray a class of people who had not had the time to accustom themselves to the privileges flowing from their power and who had not yet found the leisure in which to enjoy a pause in the fraught struggle to consolidate their position. For we are talking here not of an ossified establishment . . . whose days were numbered and which had had the time to prepare for its end. It was an end without preparation, a death without fanfare. Entirely new luxury paired with a cold death.[52]

Lenin and Stalin aimed to remake human beings on a new model. The Leviathan they created bred an elite of Hobbesian survivors, then killed them.

A fatal butterfly net

... of things impossible, which we think possible, we may deliberate, not knowing it is in vain.

Leviathan, Chapter 6

The death of the poet, children's author and fiction writer Daniil Kharms (1905–42) was played out on the margins of the Leningrad siege. A leading figure in the city's cultural avant-garde in the late twenties, he aimed to make his life an absurdist work of art. As part of the performance, he used to walk about Leningrad carrying a butterfly net.

Kharms was a member of the OBERIU (Union of Real Art) group, which included some of the poets who continued to write secretly during the blockade. His work survived almost by accident. Some months after he was arrested for the last time, his friend the philosopher Yakov Druskin (1902–80) trudged for many hours to Kharms's apartment and retrieved a suitcase stuffed with manuscripts. Carrying this with him when he evacuated the city and preserving it after he returned, he showed the contents to scholars in the 1960s.

In his prime Kharms devoted himself to self-expression. He had many friends and lovers, but seems to have lived for himself alone. His absurdism soon became dangerous.

Arrested in 1931 and 1938 for anti-Soviet tendencies, Kharms was arrested again on 23 August 1941, two months after the German invasion, on a charge of defeatism, which carried the death penalty. Denounced by an informer, most likely one of his friends, he was taken into custody. A search in the NKVD headquarters revealed that he carried a number of items with him, including his passport, marriage certificate, medical records, a poem, a copy of the New Testament, two cigarette cases, and two bronze icons as well as a wooden one, all of which were confiscated. Later the same day his apartment was searched, and notebooks, letters and a photo were removed.

During his interrogation Kharms denied committing any crimes against the Soviet state. On 2 September he was moved from the detention centre to the psychiatric wing of the NKVD hospital for psychological testing. A medical report noted that Kharms 'thinks clearly, correctly oriented with respect to time place and surroundings' but 'expresses floridly delusional notions', which are 'characterized by absurdities . . . devoid of consistency and logic'. He may have been feigning insanity in the belief that he would be spared the firing squad and the hope that in hospital he could avoid dying of starvation. On 5 December 1941 he was judged a danger to society and himself and confined in the prison hospital for mandatory treatment.

In mid-December he was transferred to the psychiatric wing of Leningrad's Prison Number One. His wife, Marina Malich, used to leave small food packages for him. When she visited the prison for the last time, on 7 February 1942, the clerk at the window asked her to wait and the window was slammed shut. When it reopened several minutes later, Marina was told: 'Passed away on the second of February.' The packet of food she brought was thrown back at her.[53]

Kharms anticipated his end in a poem he wrote in 1937:

This is how hunger begins:
you wake early and full of life

but soon begin to weaken;
the onset of boredom arrives, the sense of loss impending
of quickening powers of mind, followed by a peace descending.
And then, the terrifying ending.[54]

Kharms' place of burial is unknown.

Unlike her husband, Marina was a survivor. After he died she escaped the blockaded city. Captured by the Nazis, she was sent to Germany as a slave labourer. Escaping again, this time to France, she reconnected with her mother, who had abandoned her as a child and was then living in Nice. Seducing and marrying her mother's husband, she left Europe with him for Venezuela, where they parted and she set up a bookstore with a Russian of aristocratic background who was working as a taxi driver.

In a short story based on these events, Polina Barskova writes:

Her mother, who had left the girl behind several revolutions and wars ago, somewhat stung by her daughter's adroitness, puts on her lipstick, arranges the netting on her hat, and with firm steps (though her ankles aren't what they used to be, they're thicker now) walks to the Soviet consulate to ask them to send her daughter back – if possible to a Siberian labour camp.[55]

Marina is reported to have died in the US, in Atlanta, Georgia, in 2002.

'I am interested only in pure nonsense, only in that which has no practical meaning. I am interested in life only in its absurd manifestation.'[56] For Kharms, absurdity meant a life of playful freedom. The performance ended by killing him.

Almost nothing

That which gives to human actions the relish of justice, is a certain nobleness or gallantness of courage, (rarely found,) by which a man scorns to be beholding for the contentment of his life, to fraud, or breach of promise.

Leviathan, Chapter 15

On the morning of 2 September 1939, the Polish painter Józef Czapski, then forty-three years old, slipped a slim volume of the memoirs of André Gide into his greatcoat pocket and headed off to fight against invading Nazi forces. In a secret protocol to the Nazi–Soviet pact, formalized on 23 August, Stalin and Hitler agreed that the Polish state would be destroyed and its territory and people divided between them. Sixteen days after the German invasion, Soviet troops entered Poland from the east. Surrounded by German and Soviet forces at Lviv, Czapski's unit surrendered. The Germans turned over the Polish forces to the Soviets, and he began two years of incarceration in Soviet camps.

Though he did not know it, he and the others held prisoner with him were marked down for death. In March 1940 the head of the NKVD (later KGB), Lavrenti Beria, and three members of the Politburo signed a memorandum in which the Polish prisoners were condemned to execution by shooting. The operation, which was completed in eight weeks, began with the prisoners being transported to sites in and around Katyn, a forest near the Russian city of Smolensk. In all around 22,000 – mostly officers who in civilian life had been lawyers, doctors, writers, artists, scientists, engineers and the like – were shot by a bullet in the back of the head. The purpose of the massacre, which killed a significant section of Poland's military, political, intellectual and professional elites, was to inflict irreparable damage on the nation and prevent an independent Polish state being rebuilt.

Over a twenty-eight-day period one man, Vasily M. Blokhin (1895–1955), the chief executioner at Lubyanka prison in Moscow, where he killed the writer Isaac Babel and the avant-garde theatre director Vsevolod Meyerhold, shot around 7,000 prisoners. He used German revolvers, which he brought with him in a suitcase, as he found the Soviet-made variety un-reliable. For his services to the Soviet state Blokhin received the Order of the Red Banner. Retiring after Stalin's death, he was stripped of his rank. When he died at the age of sixty, having suffered from alcoholism for many years, the cause of death was recorded as suicide.

For reasons he never discovered, Czapski was among 395 prisoners who were not sent for execution. He was released in September 1941, when Stalin amnestied his Polish prisoners so they could fight his former Nazi ally after the German invasion of the Soviet Union in June of that year. Joining up with a new division of the Polish army composed of released Gulag pris-oners, Czapski set about trying to find the truth about the officers, travelling to Moscow as an envoy of the Polish government-in-exile in London to question NKVD officials.

Born in Prague in 1896 into a wealthy family, Czapski gradu-ated in the law faculty of the University of St Petersburg. As a young man he was a disciple of Leo Tolstoy and believed in non-violent resistance to evil. He tried to found a pacifist com-mune in Petersburg after the Bolshevik revolution, in which he and his family lost everything, but spent most of his days searching for food. In May 1918 he moved to Warsaw in newly emancipated Poland to study art. He went on to spend eight years in Paris, exchanging ideas with French and Russian artists and writers, forming passionate attachments with women and men (including one with Vladimir Nabokov's younger brother Sergei, who would perish in a Nazi camp where gay men were subjected to hideous medical experiments) and devoting himself to painting in the style of Cézanne.

Czapski made light of his time in the Gulag. An account by a fellow prisoner describes him lying in a primitive prison hospital, a long, emaciated figure – he was six and a half foot tall – blue-lipped and coughing blood, whispering passages he remembered from Proust. He was determined his days in confinement would not be wasted. He made pencil drawings and paintings on scraps of paper. Not much bigger than postage stamps, many of them depicted life in the camp, including some self-portraits. Others were miniature recreations of his pre-war paintings, left behind in a studio in Warsaw, where most of them disappeared in the course of the war.

It was in the camp, without access to Proust's writings, that Czapski gave the talks printed in *Lost Time*.[57] Czapski was not the only Gulag inmate to find in Proust a window to another world. Varlam Shalamov writes of discovering a copy of *Le Côté de Guermantes* at the bottom of a package of clothing sent to a doctor in his camp. 'Proust,' he wrote, 'was more precious than sleep.'[58] The book was stolen after he put it on a bench while talking with another prisoner.

Delivered in the evenings of the winter of 1940–41 in the refectory of a former convent that served as the prison camp's mess hall, with an audience of around forty fellow prisoners who had worked outdoors all day in temperatures as low as minus forty-five degrees, Czapski's talks are unlike anything else that has been written on Proust. He emphasizes the writer's detachment from *haute bourgeois* society and his dispassionate analysis of the vagaries of the human heart. But the core of Czapski's analysis is Proust's account of the indifference to death that comes when the mind is filled with memories that seem to come from out of time.

In a stroke of genius, Czapski compared Proust with Pascal. The author of the *Pensées* may seem an odd lens through which to view Proust. 'Devoured by a yearning for the absolute', Pascal 'considered all the ephemeral joys of the senses unacceptable'. For Proust, only the joys of the senses had value. In a letter to a friend, he confessed he wanted only one thing: to take pleasure in life, especially in sexual love. Yet, as Czapski writes, Proust's work 'leaves us with a Pascalian taste of ash in our mouths'.

Proust's novel is a meditation on the vanity of life. Swann, 'the perfect man of the world', receives a sentence of death from his doctors. When he tries to pass on the news to aristocratic friends, they tell the quaking figure he looks marvellous, then leave him standing in front of their magnificent town house as they walk off talking of the mismatch between the duchess's shoes and her ruby necklace. Odette, the beguiling courtesan who captivates Swann, appears in the final volume as a 'human wreck' ignored by guests. When Proust's narrator hears of the death of Albertine, the young girl whose radiant image enchanted him, he is busy with other matters and barely notices.

There is a crucial difference, noted by Czapski, between Pascal and Proust. Whereas Pascal turns from the world with disgust, Proust seeks salvation in its sensations. Born and buried a Catholic, carrying a small oilcloth Bible with him when he travelled through Russia in search of his fellow prisoners, Czapski was himself a religious man. He was right to discern a kind of religion in Proust's novel: a struggle to defy time and disillusion and eternalize the passing moment in images of beauty.

Czapski recounted his travels in the Soviet Union in his memoir *Inhuman Land*. Unlike many Western travellers to the Soviet Union before and after him, Czapski – who was fluent in Russian – engaged with ordinary people whenever he could. Soviet propaganda told of a country of plenty, or at least suffi-ciency. What he found was nearly universal deprivation, endured with impotent anger and despairing resignation. The German civilians he came across in his travels were no differ-ent. He describes an old woman he met in a third-class carriage of a train:

Her shoes were made of rawhide, and she had a dull, haggard complexion and the terrified eyes of a beaten dog ... This woman had always lived in Russia, and like a large number of Germans was entirely assimilated there. She lived in a small Ukrainian town where she gave German language lessons and worked at an institution for the deaf and dumb. She was on her way to Germany, a place with which she had almost no con-nection. Hitler did not exist for her; all she knew was that she was leaving Russia. Once we were in Poland, in the empty carriage, she told me about it in a whisper. It was nothing remarkable, just everyday fare for anyone who had ever been to Russia as more than a tourist: she told me that when Kirov was assassinated, the next day hundreds and hundreds of people had been deported to an unknown destination ... Several dozen people had been taken from one of the factories, loaded onto open railcars and driven dozens of miles in severe frost. They were packed in so tight there was only room to stand; most of them had no warm clothing, and when the railcars reached their destination they had to be carried out like wooden logs. Many had frozen to death.

Czapski concludes: 'She was a shadow of herself as she told me this story on the train, her eyes flashing with terror.'[59] His tone is restrained and almost calm. Episodes of the sort the old woman reported were commonplace at the time.

While in Moscow, Czapski looked in bookshops for relics of a world that had passed away. He found a beautifully bound 1868 edition of Baudelaire's *Les Fleurs du mal*, which he bought for ten roubles. (A pound of butter would have cost thirty roubles.) He met the poet Anna Akhmatova, whose husband, Nikolay Gumilov, had been shot in 1921. She 'wore a dress made of very poor material, somewhere between a sack and a pale habit . . . and spoke little, in a slightly strange tone, as if half joking, even about the saddest things'.

Czapski's attempt to discover what had happened to his fellow officers yielded nothing. Mass graves were reported near Katyn in 1942 and 1943, and used in Nazi propaganda in an attempt to split the Allies. The Polish government raised the issue with the American and British authorities, who colluded with the Soviets in denying any knowledge of the killings. For the rest of his long life (he died at the age of ninety-six) Czapski was troubled by why he had not been shot along with his fellow prisoners.

Beyond this tragedy and his painting, what mattered most to him was Ludwik Hering, whom he called his 'most important and personal living connection'. Czapski and Hering were separated by the start of the Second World War, but the two men corresponded for thirty years, writing hundreds of letters to one another. Having worked during the Nazi occupation as a nightwatchman in a tannery near the Warsaw Ghetto, Hering wrote a story about the 1943 uprising, ending with the words: 'the ruins of the ghetto tremble like printed words on a piece of paper that is coming apart.' After the story appeared in 1946, he stopped writing.

When they met again in Paris in 1972, Czapski tried to lift his friend from despair. Much of their time together was spent arguing about Dostoevsky's *Demons*, with Czapski claiming that the novel kept open the possibility of a meaningful life and Hering countering that it left no hope. In 1984, suffering from cancer, Hering killed himself. Czapski drew a line through the entry in his journal where he recorded his friend's death. But he left the entry legible, preserving his sense of loss and his gratitude for what his friend had given him.

Living in a modest studio in Paris, Czapski was producing paintings saturated with light and colour into his late eighties. Asked why his work featured 'lonely people, deserted café tables, faces half concealed in the metro, minute daily events glimpsed in passing', he replied: 'Each time, it is almost nothing. But that "almost nothing" signifies everything.'

What this meant becomes clearer in a short piece recounting Czapski's travels on trains when he was searching for his comrades:

Those days, torn from a feverish routine, from obsessive activity, I now remember as happy ones. Is there any place, any Gehenna, where a man freed from physical suffering, hunger and cold, or even from the feverishly harried responsibility for work, would not be capable of experiencing a quarter of an hour of happiness? . . . In the warm, contented compartment, I looked through the icy windows at the red sun setting, the snowdrifts that stopped us every so many dozens of hours, blocking the tracks, the ruined domes of churches with broken crosses standing in black villages and then in the steppe beyond the Volga, a snowy desert . . . almost without buildings, almost without people . . .[60]

Czapski's capacity for happiness was one of his greatest gifts. When he was buried the grave had to be lengthened, more than once, to accommodate the specially built coffin his mourners had made for him.

Silver shoes and a coat with a bullet hole

No man laughs at old jests; or weeps for an old calamity.

Leviathan, Chapter 6

A famous Russian writer, fleeing the Bolshevik Revolution and the Civil War, describes scrubbing the deck of a battered steamship while wearing silver shoes. Like the other women on board, she was saving her everyday clothes for later. Knowing it would be impossible to buy anything when they went ashore, they were wearing only things for which there was no longer any need: beautiful shawls, ball gowns, satin slippers. When she was told to do her share of the work of cleaning the ship, she did it wearing her silver shoes. Other passengers told her she cleaned badly and looked too happy when she was scrubbing.

The writer, who called herself Teffi, boarded the steamer in Odessa after a dangerous journey from Moscow through Ukraine. She crossed a country that was being fought over by the Red Army, the anti-Bolshevik Whites, a Ukrainian nationalist Green army and a Black Army of peasant anarchists. Hosts of gangsters and bandits added to the disorder. Between 1918 and 1920, the capital Kiev changed hands over a dozen times, each marked by firing squads. Teffi travelled through a zone of violence in which the daily struggle was to survive or escape.

When she reached a village that had been taken over by the Bolsheviks, she and her companions were informed they would be allowed to cross the border into Ukraine only if they helped the village commissar stage a series of theatrical events in the Club of Enlightenment and Culture. The commissar was wearing a magnificent beaver coat, which 'trailed behind him like a royal mantle in some throne-room portrait'. She noticed there was a bullet-hole in the coat, fringed with dried blood.[61] Later, she saw a dog running off with a human arm. In the end the theatrical events went off well enough, despite the top brass in the people's guardians turning up in leather jackets with bullet belts and revolvers. She was relieved to leave the village behind and continue her journey.

Before the revolution Teffi was one of the best-known writers in Russia. Born in 1872 as Nadezhda Alexandrovna Lokhvitskaya into the family of a Petersburg lawyer, she married a Polish landowner. After nearly ten years she left him to launch her career as a writer. She chose her pseudonym, she said, because it sounded like the name of a dog or a fool. By the time of the revolution she was so famous that perfumes and confectionery were branded with her pseudonym.

She knew everybody. She writes of spending an evening with Rasputin, the peasant mystic who had become almost a member of the family of Tsar Nicholas II (one of Teffi's most avid readers). She describes Rasputin as being swept away in a whirlwind, deliriously repeating to himself: 'God . . . prayer . . . wine.'

She also knew Lenin. Leaning left in her sympathies, she worked for a while for the first Bolshevik newspaper to be openly published in Russia. She describes the Bolshevik as being simple in his manner and having no feeling at all for beauty. He was not an orator who could set a crowd on fire: he 'simply battered away with a blunt instrument at the darkest corner of people's souls, where greed, spite and cruelty lay hidden'.[62] (Teffi was not the only one who found Lenin's oratory unappealing. The Russian composer Nicolas Nabokov, first cousin of the writer Vladimir Nabokov, was taken by his tutor in April 1917 to hear Lenin speak. Nabokov recalled him addressing a handful of people in his 'shrill, high-pitched voice, rolling his r's in the manner of upper-class salon snobs, using many "barbarisms", words of foreign extraction gleaned from the West European vocabulary'.[63])

As Teffi saw him, Lenin was just a vehicle of a political idea. 'Possessed maniacs of this kind' she concluded 'are truly terrifying'. When he closed down the cultural section of the paper because it was of no practical use in the revolutionary struggle, she resigned her position.

In the course of her travels Teffi witnessed many terrifying scenes. What is remarkable is the lightness of touch with which she records them. She expects little of the people she encounters. Acquaintances who declared themselves her dearest friends promised to take her on the next leg of her perilous journey, then casually departed without her. She writes of these incidents without bitterness or self-pity. 'People are just carrying on their lives, living the way they have always lived, as is their human nature.'[64]

Ending up in Paris in 1919, she continued writing on a bedside table in a small room near Montparnasse station. Aside from expressing her horror at Nazism, which she lived long enough to witness – she died in 1952 – she published nothing on politics during the rest of her life. The shifts of events were a comedy, at times too cruel for laughter. 'Life inside a joke,' Teffi wrote, 'is more tragic than funny.'[65]

The final impression Teffi leaves on the reader is not one of sadness. A Russian critic, the émigré poet Georgy Adamovich, wrote: 'There are writers who muddy their own water, in order to make it seem deeper. Teffi could not be more different: the water is entirely transparent, yet the bottom is barely visible.'[66] At the bottom there was absurdity, and it may have been this that kept her alive.

The first dystopia

It is true, that certain living creatures, as bees, and ants, live sociably one with another, (which are therefore by Aristotle numbered amongst political creatures;) and yet have no other direction, than their particular judgments and appetites; nor speech, whereby one of them can signify to another, what he thinks expedient for the common benefit: and therefore some man may perhaps desire to know, why mankind cannot do the same.

Leviathan, Chapter 17

In May 1929, the Soviet author Yevgeny Zamyatin was the target of hostile verses composed by the poet Aleksandr Bezymensky, a member of the Russian Association of Proletarian Writers. Appearing in the Leningrad edition of the prestigious *Literary Gazette* under the title 'Certificate Concerning Social Eugenics', one of the ditties read:

Type: Zamyatin.
Genus: Evgeny.
Class: bourgeois.
In the village: a kulak.
The product of degeneration.
Footnote: an enemy.

With its references to degeneration, this sinister doggerel would not have been out of place in *Der Stürmer*, the Nazi tabloid that was being published in Germany at the time. The attack was the culmination of a campaign that made Zamyatin's position in the country untenable. In September 1929 he resigned from the Soviet Union of Writers, and in early June 1931 wrote to Stalin asking permission to emigrate. Supported by Maxim Gorky, Zamyatin's request was granted. Accompanied by his wife, Lyudmila, he left Russia and settled in Paris, where he died of a heart attack in 1937.

More than anyone else, it was George Orwell who made Zamyatin known in the West. Reviewing Zamyatin's masterpiece *We* in 1946, he referred to it as 'one of the literary curiosities of this book-burning age'. In one respect, Orwell's review may have had the effect of diminishing Zamyatin's achievement. He believed the book was written around the time of Lenin's death in 1924. In fact, as Zamyatin's biographer has shown,[67] it was written in 1918–19, the years in which the Bolsheviks launched their first wave of terror. *We* is not so much a clairvoyant anticipation of the future as an unblinking insight into Zamyatin's present, when the totalitarian logic of the Soviet project was already unfolding.

Astutely, Orwell linked *We* with Aldous Huxley's *Brave New World* (1932). Huxley envisaged a world from which freedom had been almost eradicated for the sake of maximizing happiness. Orwell rated Zamyatin's dystopia superior to Huxley's on account of its 'intuitive grasp of the irrational side of totalitarianism – human sacrifice, cruelty as an end in itself, the worship of a leader who is credited with divine attributes'. These elements are present in *Nineteen Eighty-Four* (published in 1949), which Orwell admitted was influenced by Zamyatin's novel.

We is the first fully developed dystopia. H. G. Wells, with whom Zamyatin had several meetings when Wells visited the Soviet Union in 1920 and on whose work he wrote a long essay, produced some memorable dystopias. In his first novel, *The Time Machine* (1895), the delicate Eloi lead a charmed life based on the slave labour of the subterranean Morlocks. *The Island of Dr Moreau* (1896) pictures the creation of hideous and wretched hybrid species – a theme prefigured in Mary Shelley's *Franken-stein* (1818). In *The Iron Heel* (1908), the American socialist writer Jack London – whose work Zamyatin translated into Russian – tells of a hyper-capitalist oligarchy coming to power in the United States. E. M. Forster's 'The Machine Stops' (1909) has humans living underground, their needs provided for by an omnipotent Machine, whose breakdown signals the end of their world. Yet none of these contain the central theme of dystopian fiction, which is the revolt of human passions against totalitarian order.

Born in 1884 in Lebedian, around 300 kilometres from Moscow, his father an Orthodox priest, his mother a musician, Zamyatin always lived parallel lives. A rebel against tsarism, he joined the Bolshevik faction of the Russian Social Democratic Labour party as a student. During the revolutionary distur-bances of 1905 he was a clandestine activist, hiding pamphlets and weapons while training as a maritime engineer in the Poly-technic Institute in St Petersburg, spending three months in solitary confinement after he was discovered and imprisoned.

Travelling across Russia inspecting ports and submarines, he simultaneously established himself as a writer by publishing a number of short stories. He continued to pursue a dual career when he was sent to Tyneside to supervise the building of ice-breakers for the Russian Imperial Navy. Living in Newcastle, he produced *The Islanders*, where he parodied the class system of provincial Edwardian England. He went on to adopt the tweedy suits and reserved manner of the country he satirized, so much so that his Russian contemporaries nicknamed him 'the Englishman'.

Zamyatin's independence soon brought him into conflict with the Bolshevik authorities. Within weeks of the October Revolution of 1917, he was denouncing the Soviet state for its dictatorial methods. Perceived as a potential enemy, he was arrested and interrogated by the Cheka in February 1919, then again in March and May, under suspicion of colluding with members of the Social Revolutionary party in a supposed plot against the regime.

The danger he faced became clear when in August 1921 his friend the avant-garde literary theorist Nikolai Gumilev was arrested for involvement in a trumped-up monarchist conspiracy, sentenced to death and shot with sixty others in the Kovalesky Forest not far from St Petersburg. (An estimated 4,500 victims of the campaign of terror in which Gumilev was killed are buried in unmarked graves at the site.)

In 1922, Zamyatin spent a month in prison during a crackdown that culminated in the mass expulsion of some the country's leading intellectuals in 'the philosophers' steamships'.[68] Some believed it was Trotsky who singled out Zamyatin for deportation. After the ships had sailed, Zamyatin's deportation was discussed by other leading Bolsheviks, including the Commissar of Enlightenment, Anatoly Lunarcharsky, who oversaw censorship of the arts. In the event, Zamyatin was not expelled. For some years he wavered as to whether he should join the Russian writers who had gone abroad. Though he attacked the Bolsheviks from the time they seized power, he declined to join any of the émigré factions when he arrived in Paris. He was as independent abroad as he had been in the Soviet Union.

Written as forty 'records' by 'D-503', a mathematician and engineer, *We* describes a society governed by the dictates of reason. With every aspect of their lives controlled, including the allocation of sexual partners, citizens of the One State live in glass houses that enable continuous surveillance. Their behaviour is regulated by what we would call algorithms – mathematical formulae that prescribe how every hour of the day could be most efficiently spent. A Green Wall seals them off from fur-clothed primitives who live beyond the city. Looming over this closed society, an all-seeing Benefactor ensures that its harmonious functioning continues undisturbed.

D-503 meets a free-spirited woman, I-330, to whom he is strongly attracted. Instead of the medicinal sex prescribed by the State, they form a passionate relationship. I-330 reveals she is involved with the Mephi, an organization dedicated to tearing down the Wall. D-503 decides to report her to the Guardians, but cannot bring himself to do it.

The last record has D-503 recovering from a 'Great Operation' in which his capacity for emotion has been flattened:

> . . . now I am healthy: I am completely and totally healthy. I'm smiling: I can't help smiling: a splinter has been removed from my head and now it is empty and light.

He informs on his lover and watches her being tortured without feeling sympathy or remorse. Unlike Julia in Orwell's *Nineteen Eighty-Four*, I-330 refuses to betray her co-conspirators. Unbroken, she is executed along with them. The Green Wall is penetrated, and sectors of the city are littered with dead bodies. D-503 is unperturbed. 'I'm certain: we'll win. For reason must win in the end.'

Zamyatin did not object to Utopia because it is unrealizable.

He would reject it all the more if it could be achieved. Any Utopia must be dystopian, for a life of rational harmony is the death of the soul.

Bukharin's confession and fear of the dark

And as the last appetite in deliberation is called the *will* ; so the last opinion in search of the truth of past, and future, is called the JUDGMENT, or *resolute* and *final sentence* of him that discourseth.

Leviathan, Chapter 8

Nikolai Bukharin made the following confession during his final plea before the Supreme Court of the USSR on the evening of 12 March 1938:

I am guilty of treason to the socialist fatherland, the most heinous of possible crimes, of the organization of kulak uprisings, of preparations for terrorist acts, and of belonging to an underground, anti-Soviet organization. I further admit I am guilty of organizing a conspiracy for a 'palace coup' . . . I consider myself responsible for a grave and monstrous crime against the socialist fatherland and the whole international proletariat . . . While in prison I made a re-evaluation of my entire past. For when you ask yourself: 'If you must die, what are you dying for?' an absolutely black vacuity suddenly rises before you with startling vividness . . . I am perhaps speaking for the last time in my life.[69]

Bukharin's confession was the inspiration for Arthur Koestler's novel *Darkness at Noon*. First translated by Koestler's girlfriend, the sculptor Daphne Hardy, when the pair were living together in Paris and smuggled by Hardy out of France, the novel was first published in English in London in December 1940 during the Blitz. The unforgettable title echoing a passage in the Book of Job – 'They meet with darkness in the daytime, and grope in the noonday as in the night' – was chosen by Hardy. Arriving in Britain in November 1940 after being interned in a French camp, escaping France by joining and deserting from the Foreign Legion, Koestler was in Pentonville gaol as an illegal immigrant when the book appeared. It soon became an international best-seller.

It requires an effort of historical imagination to enter into the ideological passions that surrounded communism. Viewing Koestler's masterpiece as a relic of another era, however, misses its lasting significance. The psychology of the political believer is not confined to interwar communists and fellow travellers. The same mixture of self-deception and adamant certainty can be observed in post-Cold War liberals. They too cannot admit the demise of the faith that has given meaning to their lives.

Koestler's protagonist, Nikolai Salmanovich Rubashov, a veteran communist facing execution as a traitor to the Soviet cause, was modelled on Bukharin, whom Koestler had met when he visited the Soviet Union in 1932. Bukharin was arraigned in the show trials that followed the murder of Sergei Kirov, the head of the communist party in Leningrad, in December 1934, by an embittered former party employee. Some suspect Stalin arranged Kirov's death, but possibly he only exploited it for his own ends. Either way, the Great Purge he launched claimed somewhere in the region of three quarters of a million lives.

Bukharin's confession came after a year of imprisonment

and interrogation. While in gaol he was not idle. He produced four book-length manuscripts, including nearly 180 poems, a memoir in the form of a novel and two works of Marxian theory – altogether some 1,400 typewritten pages. He wrote at night or in intervals between interrogation sessions, in the hope that after his execution the papers would be passed on to his wife Anna Larina, who could then edit and publish them.

Bukharin never doubted that he would be executed, but he did try to influence how he would be killed. His last letter to Stalin in December 1937 contained a plea for an 'act of mercy': rather than being shot by a bullet in the back of the head, he begged to be allowed to take poison. In response, Stalin ordered that when he was executed on 15 March 1938 Bukharin be given a chair from which he could watch as sixteen co-defendants were shot, one by one, until he was himself shot in the back of the head.[70]

Stalin buried Bukharin's papers in his personal archives. He was rehabilitated in 1988 during Gorbachev's perestroika and his writings unearthed in 1992, so Anna lived to see them published. The humanistic socialism of which Bukharin dreamt remained a mirage as it had been during his lifetime. Three years after Anna died in 1996, Vladimir Putin was appointed acting prime minister of the Russian Federation by Boris Yeltsin and named by Yeltsin as his successor.

Why Bukharin confessed to the crimes of which he was accused is central to his significance today. Koestler had Bukharin's alter-ego Rubashov accepting the accusations against him as a final act of loyalty to the party. Some of Koestler's contemporaries regarded this as nonsense. The Polish-Jewish poet, sometime communist and later convert to Catholicism Aleksander Wat, who had been arrested, interrogated and interned in Soviet prisons, wrote that for most of those who admitted to

crimes they had never committed, the mild methods of interrogation described in *Darkness at Noon* 'would have been the
subject of gay mockery'. Wat took his own life in Paris in 1967.[71]

In the show trials the extraction of confessions was a mech-
anical process in which the will of the accused was methodically
broken. There was the 'conveyor' system in which prisoners
were beaten for days or weeks on end by warders working in
shifts, joined with psychological coercion – sleep deprivation,
mock executions and the like. In his landmark biography,
Bukharin and the Bolshevik Revolution (1971), Stephen Cohen
maintained that Bukharin was probably not tortured. Evidence
surfacing in the late 1980s suggests he most likely had at least
been threatened with torture. There were also threats to the
prisoners' families, like that to which Bukharin surrendered
when, around 2 June 1937, his interrogators told him they
would have his wife, Anna Larina, and their newborn son killed
if he did not submit. It was then that he signed his confession,
naming forty-two other conspirators in the 'palace coup', most
of whom had already been arrested. His wife and son were
consigned to camps and orphanages. Anna had her one remaining photograph of her son confiscated, and it was another
twenty years before they met again.

Remarkably, Bukharin's will was not broken. His performance at the trial was a tour de force of self-defence and
counter-attack. Now that it seemed all was lost, he appeared
determined to assert himself in the face of overwhelming odds.

Though a written record remains, no frame of film or photograph showing the faces of the defendants in the trials has
survived. In some ways this is surprising. The Soviet authorities had little reason to fear world opinion. Many Western
liberals were convinced the trials and confessions were genu-
ine. An open letter was circulated by the American humanist

philosopher Corliss Lamont appealing for signatures in support of the trial. The *New York Times*, the *Nation*, the *New Republic* and the American ambassador Joseph Davies were all ready to believe the defendants were guilty of attempting to mount a *coup d'etat* against the Soviet regime. Progressive intellectuals rallied to defend Stalin against the powerless and doomed Bukharin.

Koestler's belief that Bukharin confessed willingly was mistaken. Like the other defendants, he did so only under extreme duress. Yet Koestler was right when he had Rubashov, nearing execution, admitting that he and the other Old Bolsheviks were guilty of other crimes they could not admit:

> They were too deeply woven into their own past, caught in the web they had so assiduously spun according to their circuitous logic and convoluted morality; they were all guilty, just not of the particular misdeeds to which they were confessing. For them there was no turning back.[72]

All the defendants had consigned innocent people to prison or death in the service of the Bolshevik cause, then covered up their crimes. In the inner-party conflicts of the twenties, Bukharin sided with Stalin against his fellow Old Bolsheviks Lev Kamenev and Grigory Zinoviev, who were also executed after show trials. He questioned some of the worst Soviet crimes, such as the repression of the Kronstadt sailors' rebellion by Lenin and his War Commissar, Trotsky, in 1921, and the war Stalin waged on the peasants when he imposed collectivization. But there is no record of Bukharin protesting when, in a letter in August 1918, Lenin ordered that hundreds of sex workers he believed were demoralizing Soviet troops be deported or shot. Bukharin said nothing when Lenin issued his 'Hanging Order', a few days later, in a telegram to the Bolsheviks of Penza province directing them to publicly hang a hundred 'kulaks' so that the peasants who were resisting grain requisition would 'see, tremble' and submit.[73] Bukharin was silently complicit in the first wave of mass Soviet terror in September 1918, during which some 10,000–15,000 people were executed.

Along with his fellow Bolsheviks, Bukharin endorsed the founding constitution of the Soviet state, which created a category of 'former persons', human remnants of the old order who were denied civic rights, including the rations needed to sustain life. When innocents were executed or starved to death because they were not needed in the new society, Bukharin showed no signs of regret. If they were accused of impossible crimes, he pretended to believe in their guilt.

Bolshevism with a human face was never more than a phantom. Yet there is no evidence Bukharin ever asked himself the question posed by Isaac Babel in his *1920 Diary*, written when he was fighting in the Red Army, two decades before Stalin had him shot in Lubyanka prison: 'We are the vanguard, but of what?'[74]

Koestler understood the Bolshevik mind because he too had concealed the truth for the cause. He spent the winter of 1932–3 in Kharkiv, then capital of Soviet Ukraine. He had been commissioned by the Moscow-based International Organisation of Revolutionary Writers to write a book, *Russia through Bourgeois Eyes*, recounting how a liberal Western journalist was turned into an admirer of Soviet progress after visiting the country.

Koestler arrived in the USSR at the peak of the Holodomor, the politically engineered famine in which 4 million or more were starved to death. Travelling by train through the countryside, he found 'the stations were lined with begging peasants with swollen hands and feet, the women holding up to the carriage-windows horrible infants with enormous wobbling heads, stick-like limbs, swollen, pointed bellies'. When he witnessed these scenes Koestler was working as a member of the intelligence service of the Comintern, the Third Communist International, founded in 1919. The articles he submitted to Moscow were eulogies to the rapid advances being made under the Five-Year Plan. The famine was not mentioned. Koestler severed his links with the party in 1938, but it was years later, in a section of his book of essays *The Yogi and the Commissar* (1945) and memoirs published in the fifties, that he wrote of what he had seen.

Koestler was able to produce the greatest fictional account of the Soviet system because – unlike George Orwell – he succumbed, for a time, to the totalitarian temptation. For him, communism was more than a political project. It made sense of the chaos around him, and his life became more than simply a moment in a nightmare.

In 1937, working as a journalist in Spain, Koestler was captured by Franco's forces and imprisoned as a spy under sentence of death. (He escaped execution via a prisoner swap.) While in gaol, he experienced an epiphany in which he became convinced that 'a higher reality existed, and that it alone invested existence with meaning'. The universe was a text written in invisible ink that pointed to a realm outside of time and history.

In the years following the Second World War, Koestler was an active anti-communist, but by the fifties his interest in politics was waning. He was active in humanitarian causes, such as the abolition of capital punishment and securing educational opportunities for prisoners, but his chief focus was in exploring what might lie beyond the reductive materialism he accepted during his years as a communist. He developed a strong interest in heterodox science, and left a bequest for the establishment of a professorship in parapsychology.

Along with five others, Koestler chronicled his disillusion-
ment in an essay collection, *The God That Failed* (1950), edited by
the Labour politician Richard Crossman. Most ex-communists
went on to become liberals of one kind or another. When the
Soviet state imploded, their conversion seemed vindicated. But
Koestler believed the malaise of contemporary societies was
too deep to be cured by another dose of liberalism, a view subsequent events have shown to be well-founded.

A global liberal order is more distant than it has ever been. Yet,
in the aftermath of the Russian invasion of a European land,
Western countries were congratulating themselves on their unity.
A second end of history, which had failed to materialize when
Fukuyama announced it in 1989, had seemingly arrived. In fact, a
curtain had dropped like that which came down over Russia in
1917, leaving the prospects of the liberal West doubtful.

Unlike humanistic Bolshevism, liberal societies did once
exist. But they came into being by accident, and there was never
any possibility they would become universal. Today they are
themselves ceasing to be liberal. In the midst of these realities,
the moth-eaten musical brocade of progressive hope has been
rolled out again. Without the pattern they believe to be unfolding in history, twenty-first-century liberals – like Bukharin – face
'an absolutely black vacuity'.

It would be wiser to admit, as Koestler did in regard to communism, that the post-Cold War dream of a new world order
was an illusion. But twenty-first-century liberals can no more
renounce their faith than could interwar communists: it is
necessary for their mental survival. If liberalism has a future, it
will be as therapy against fear of the dark.

3.

Mortal gods

This is the generation of that great LEVIATHAN, or rather (to speak more reverently) of that *Mortal God*, to which we owe under the *Immortal God*, our peace and defence.

Leviathan, Chapter 17

Liberalism was a creation of Western monotheism and liberal freedoms part of the civilization that monotheism engendered. Twenty-first-century liberals reject this civilization, while continuing to assert the universal authority of a hollowed-out version of its values. In this hyper-liberal vision, all societies are destined to undergo the deconstruction that is under way in the West.

Within Western societies, the hyper-liberal goal is to enable human beings to define their own identities. From one point of view this is the logical endpoint of individualism: each human being is sovereign in deciding who or what they want to be. From another, it is the project of forging new collectives, and the prelude to a state of chronic warfare among the identities they embody.

Human beings can never be wholly self-defined. If their identity is to be more than a private fantasy, they must somehow induce others to accept it. Hyper-liberals aim to achieve this by capturing institutions that divide people into distinct categories, which then become competing groups. The stakes are not only the selves that are chosen but the positions in society that go with them. The result is to make self-definition a battle for power in which words are the weapons of choice.

Woke religion and surplus elites

Their moral philosophy is but a description of their own passions.

Leviathan, Chapter 46

The origins of what has come to be called the woke movement are in the decay of liberalism. The movement is most powerful in English-speaking countries – tellingly, the countries where classical liberalism was strongest. Beyond the Anglosphere, in China, the Middle East, India, Africa and most of continental Europe, it is regarded with indifference, bemusement or contempt. While its apostles regard it as a universal movement of human emancipation, it is recognized in much of the world as a symptom of Western decline – a hyperbolic version of the liberalism the West professed during its brief period of seeming hegemony after the Cold War.

Hyper-liberal ideology plays a number of roles. It operates as a rationale for a failing variety of capitalism, and a vehicle through which surplus elites struggle to secure a position of power in society. Insofar as it expresses a coherent system of ideas, it is the anti-Western creed of an antinomian intelligentsia that is ineffably Western. Psychologically, it provides an ersatz faith for those who cannot live without the hope of universal salvation inculcated by Christianity.

Contrary to its right-wing critics, woke thinking is not a variant of Marxism. No woke ideologue comes anywhere close to Karl Marx in rigour, breadth and depth of thought. One function of woke movements is to deflect attention from the destructive impact on society of market capitalism. Once questions of identity become central in politics, conflicts of economic interests can be disregarded. Idle chatter of micro-aggression screens out class hierarchy and the abandonment of large sections of society to idleness and destitution. Flattering those who protest against slights to their well-cultivated self-image, identity politics consigns to obloquy and oblivion those whose lives are blighted by an economic system that discards them as useless.

Neither is woke thinking a version of 'post-modernism'. There is nothing in it of Jacques Derrida's playful subtlety or Michel Foucault's mordant wit. Derrida never suggested every idea should be deconstructed, nor did Foucault suppose society could do without power structures. Just as fascism debased Nietzsche's thinking, hyper-liberalism vulgarizes post-modern philosophy.

In their economic aspects, woke movements are a revolt of the professional bourgeoisie. As capitalism concentrates wealth and power in ever smaller sections of society, university professors, media figures, lawyers, charity workers, community activists and officers in non-government organizations face increasing competition, falling incomes and dwindling status. Elites have been produced in numbers greater than society can absorb. If Western capitalism creates an expanding underclass without any productive function, it also produces a lumpen intelligentsia that is economically superfluous. The result in both cases is to destabilize the political system through which this type of capitalism reproduces itself.

The role of surplus elites in politics has been examined by the historian and sociologist Peter Turchin.[1] The theory of elite overproduction continues the work of the political economist Vilfredo Pareto (1848–1923). Pareto analysed political belief systems as rationalizations of elite power struggles.[2]

Today what drives these struggles is not just rivalry for power but insecurity. Surplus elites are waging a war for economic survival in which hyper-liberal values are commodified in the labour market. Woke is a career as much as a cult. By advertising their virtue, redundant graduates hope to gain a foothold on the crumbling ladder that leads to safety as one of society's guardians.

The university campus is the model for an inquisitorial regime that has extended its reach throughout society. At the University of Illinois Urbana-Champaign, applicants seeking positions in chemical and biomolecular engineering must submit a statement 'describing the candidate's approach to an experience with diversity, equity and inclusion in higher education'. Every open faculty position listed by Ohio State University's College of Arts and Sciences, including economics, freshwater biology and astronomy, requires a statement 'articulating the applicant's demonstrated commitments and capacities to contribute to diversity, equity and inclusion through research, teaching, mentoring, and/or outreach and engagement'. The University of California Berkeley's Rubric for Assessing Candidate Contributions to Diversity, Equity, Inclusion and Belonging goes further in requiring that a low score be given to any candidate who 'states the intention of ignoring the varying backgrounds of their students and "treating everyone the same"'. Similar practices exist throughout much of American higher education.[3]

Woke thinking represents itself as a global movement in which America is taking the lead. In practice it is highly parochial. Books such as Robin D'Angelo's *White Fragility: Why It's So Hard for White People to Talk about Racism* (2018) provincialize a universal evil. A critique of racism cannot be based on twenty-first-century American theories of 'whiteness'. The Holocaust has not ceased to be an unparalleled crime because those who were murdered in it were 'white'. The Rwandan genocide of 1994 and massacres of Muslims in the Balkan wars after the breakup of Yugoslavia were racist atrocities. The Russian attempt to eradicate Ukrainian culture in occupied territories is a racist enterprise, as is the Chinese attempt to obliterate the Tibetans, the Uighurs and other minority peoples.

One of the defining features of American racism is its links with black slavery. The institution of slavery does not always come in the form of a binary type of racial oppression, however. Many forms of enslavement – based on military capture, debt or hereditary caste – existed in ancient Greece and Rome and much of the Middle East, and slave trading was practised in Africa centuries before the arrival of European colonialism. Serfdom in Russia – which was abolished in 1861, before slavery was prohibited in the US in 1865 – was not race-based, any more than was the re-enslavement of peasants in Soviet collective farms and the imposition of forced labour on millions of Gulag prisoners. In its contemporary form of human trafficking, slavery is often associated with racist practices; but the structures of power that enable it rest on inequalities that are economic as much as racial. Injustice and oppression cannot be modelled on the experience of any one society or period.

Critical Race Theory has the same defect as Samuel Huntington's theory of international relations: it projects a particular American history onto all of humankind. The late Harvard scholar's *The Clash of Civilizations and the Remaking of World Order* (1996) was not an analysis of civilizational conflicts but a contribution to an insular debate on multiculturalism. Huntington's civilizations were American minorities.

Racial oppression of black people in America is stark, extreme and enduring. The case of Sergeant Isaac Woodard is instructive. A 27-year-old African American Army veteran travelling home to his family in North Carolina on a Greyhound bus in 1946 after being discharged from service in the Second World War, Woodard asked the driver to make a stop so he could use a restroom. When the journey paused in Batesburg, South Carolina, the driver called the police, and Woodward was taken off the bus. After being led into an alleyway, he was beaten with nightsticks. He was then arrested for disorderly conduct and taken to the town jail. Along the way he was repeatedly punched in the eyes. During the night in jail the police chief continued beating him, using billy clubs to stab his eyes. The following morning Woodard appeared in court, where the judge found him guilty of the offence of which he had been charged and fined him fifty dollars. He ended up in a city hospital, where he was denied proper care, until he was moved to an army facility in Spartanburg, where doctors confirmed that his sight in both eyes had been permanently destroyed.

Woodard's case was taken up by the National Association of Colored People, and attracted the attention of President Harry Truman, who became involved after learning that Woodard was assaulted while wearing his uniform. Until Truman abolished the practice in July 1948, the American Army was racially segregated. In this regard, American forces were alone among the Allies in the Second World War. In the UK the government recommended that pubs and other meeting places ban racial mixing wherever black American troops were stationed, but official advice was widely ignored and at times actively resisted. In the Battle of Bamber Bridge, English villagers fought against

American forces that tried to enforce segregation on black soldiers.[4] The British slave trade was abolished by Act of Parliament in 1807 and slavery itself throughout the British empire in 1834, a generation before it was abolished in the US. America has been a consistent laggard in removing the worst forms of racism against black people.

After an investigation into how Woodard had been treated, the police chief was indicted. Tried before an all-white jury, he was found innocent of all charges, despite admitting that he had repeatedly bludgeoned Woodard's eyes. He died at the age of ninety-five in Batesburg, the town where he had blinded Woodard half a century earlier, in 1997. Moving to New York after the trial, Woodard died in a veteran's hospital in 1992 at the age of seventy-three.

It is hard to imagine a more potent symbol of racial injustice than the blinding of Sergeant Isaac Woodard. Yet American racism is not a paradigm for racism everywhere, nor is American multiculturalism a model any other society has reason to emulate. Carving up society into ethnic group identities perpetuates and intensifies racial divisions. Woke discourse on race is a symptom of the disease it pretends to cure.

God-building liberals

An image (in the most strict signification of the word) is the resemblance of something visible: in which sense the phantastical forms, apparitions, or seemings of visible bodies to the sight, are only *images*: such as are the show of a man, or other thing in the water, by reflection, or refraction; or of the sun, and stars by direct vision in the air; which are nothing real in the things seen, nor in the place where they seem to be; nor are their magnitudes and figures the same with that of the object; but changeable, by the variation of the organs of sight, or by glasses; and are present oftentimes in our imagination, and in our dreams, when the object is absent; or changed into other colours, and shapes, as things that only depend upon the fancy. And these are the images which are originally and most properly called *ideas*, and *idols* . . .

Leviathan, Chapter 45

In both its canonical and hyperbolic forms, liberalism is a footnote to Christianity. John Locke and his disciples avowedly derived their liberalism from Protestant Christianity. Later classical liberals were offspring of Christianity who became possessed by faith in reason. In John Stuart Mill, liberalism became a separate religion, with humankind serving as the Supreme Being, while hyper-liberals have made liberalism into a cult of self-creation.

All four of the defining ideas of liberal thought are continuations of Christian monotheism. The primacy of the individual is a secular translation of the belief that each human being is created by the Deity, which has an authority over them which transcends any worldly power. The egalitarian belief that human beings have the same moral status reproduces the idea that all human beings are equal in the sight of God. Liberal universalism – the belief that generically human attributes are more important than particular cultural identities – reflects the idea that humankind is created in God's image. The belief that human institutions are indefinitely improvable replicates the theistic faith that history is a moral narrative of sin followed by redemption.

The ancient pre-Christian world accepted that the evils of human life recur in unending cycles. The secular humanist faith in progress is a pseudo-solution to the so-called problem of evil, which arises only with belief in a benevolent and omnipotent creator-god. If there is a god supreme over all others in Hindu, Buddhist and Taoist traditions, it transcends human values. Only monotheism puts humankind at the centre of things, and only a particular strand in Western Christianity led to the human species being modelled on the Deity.

The first thinker to deify the human animal was an anti-liberal, the French founder of Positivism, Auguste Comte (1798–1857), who invented what he called the Religion of Humanity. The new creed attracted the engineers of the Panama Canal, the novelist George Eliot and the canonical liberal John Stuart Mill, who turned Comte's concoction into a secular religion that is the unwitting faith of intellectual elites throughout the West today.

In *Auguste Comte and Positivism*, a little-read and revealing essay first published in 1865 as two articles in the *Westminster Review*, Mill endorsed Comte's belief that humanity should replace God as an object of worship:

> . . . we should, with M. Comte, regard the Grand Etre, Humanity, or Mankind, as composed, in the past, solely of those who, in every age and variety of position, have played their part worthily in life. It is only as thus restricted that the aggregate of our species becomes an object deserving our veneration . . .
>
> We, therefore, not only hold that M. Comte was justified in the attempt to develope his philosophy into a religion, and had realized the essential conditions of one, but that all other religions are made better in proportion as, in their practical result, they are brought to coincide with that which he aimed at constructing.[5]

An admirer of the 'organic' society he believed existed in medieval Europe, Comte had a high regard for the Catholic Church. With the rise of science a new organic order had to be built. As knowledge increased, freedom of thought would be no more necessary in ethics and politics than in physics or chemistry. In the Religion of Humanity, tolerance is *not* a virtue.

Comte based his new religion on a new science of 'sociology', a term he invented in 1838. In his *Course of Positive Philosophy*, published in six volumes between 1830 and 1842, he used the term to describe an inquiry that would explain not only how society functioned but how it ought to function. Once values could be decided by scientific experts, the world could be delivered from ignorance.

Comte's authoritarian philosophy had a strong attraction for the European far right. Charles Maurras (1868–1952), the intellectual leader of the fascist Action Française movement – who narrowly escaped execution for collaborating with the Nazis when France was occupied by them during the Second World War – was an ardent disciple. (Despite being an atheist for most of his life, Maurras shared Comte's admiration for the Catholic Church. Unlike Comte, he doubted whether a newly designed religion could have the same authority.)

Comte's illiberalism left Mill in a quandary. Throughout his life he struggled with a conflict between progress and freedom. In *On Liberty* he proposed that a publicly funded *advocatus diaboli* be tasked with producing counter-arguments to the most widely accepted beliefs. The 'Saint of Rationalism' – as the British prime minister W. E. Gladstone called Mill – looked to the devil for salvation.[6]

Mill was an empiricist, who believed all beliefs must be subjected to the test of experience, but his empiricism never extended to his ideas about the good life. His official philosophy was a version of Utilitarianism in which all that mattered was maximizing pleasure. Yet he never doubted that the 'higher pleasures' of the mind were intrinsically more valuable than the pleasures of the body. In Utilitarianism he wrote:

> A being of higher faculties requires more to make him happy, is capable probably of more acute suffering, and is certainly accessible to it at more points, than one of an inferior type; but in spite of these liabilities, he can never really wish to sink into what he feels to be a lower grade of existence . . . It is better to be a human being dissatisfied than a pig satisfied; better to be Socrates dissatisfied than a fool satisfied.[7]

Mill promoted what he called 'experiments of living',[8] but it is unlikely that the buttoned-up Victorian sage spent much time trying out piggish pleasures. The ancient Greek hedonists of the Cyrenaic school, who did not have his inhibitions, reached a different view: 'Bodily pleasures are actually much better than pleasures of the soul, and bodily pains are worse.'[9] Mill's certainty about the good life was the fruit of inexperience.

Though he was reared by his father to have no religion, Mill inherited his way of thinking from theism. In On Liberty he tried to defend individual freedom by invoking general welfare or utility, 'the ultimate appeal on all ethical questions'. But it had to be 'utility in the largest sense, grounded on the permanent interests of man as a progressive being'.[10] Humankind progressed by developing 'individuality',[11] a style of life expressing what was unique in each person.

Just as the Romantic artist generates new visions, human beings invent new lives. In each case, they are creating something out of nothing. The idea of creation originates in Jewish religion. In ancient Greek thinking, the world is everlasting.

Plato's Forms are out of time; the visible world is a cave of flickering shadows. In the Hebrew bible, the world and the soul are created by God from nothingness. The modern ideal of self-creation, which has reached its self-destroying apotheosis in the hyper-liberal West, is forgotten theology filtered through a Romantic cult of originality.

A historian of the classical world has written:

> The tracks of Christian theology, Nietzsche had complained, wound everywhere. In the early twenty-first century, they led – as they had done in earlier ages – in various and criss-crossing directions. They led towards TV stations in which televangelists preached the headship of men over women; and they led as well to gender studies departments, in which Christianity was condemned for heteronormative marginalization of LBTQIA+. Nietzsche had foretold it all ... Any condemnation of Christianity as patriarchal and repressive derived from a framework of values that was itself utterly Christian.[12]

The pagan world admired power and glory; the weak counted for little or nothing. Christianity transvalued pagan values. A human being broken on a cross became a sign of God's love of the powerless and a guarantee of their salvation. The world would be redeemed by God's sacrifice. This Christian message inflamed the millenarian movements of medieval times and the secular revolutionaries of the twentieth century. It underpinned classical liberalism, and inspires hyper-liberals today. In woke movements, victimhood confers moral authority, as it does in Christianity. The difference is that in the Christian myth divinity joins itself with broken humanity, while woke liberals use the groups they choose as victims to enhance their own self-esteem.[13]

The link between Christianity and liberalism is not universal. Coptic, Orthodox, Roman Catholic and many contemporary varieties of Christianity have no special affinities with liberal values, or are hostile to them. Woke hyper-liberalism is Puritan moral frenzy unrestrained by divine mercy or forgiveness of sin. There is no tolerance for those who refuse to be saved.

Tolerance was the practice of living with beliefs and values believed to be heretical or wicked. An acceptance that human-kind is flawed enabled liberal societies to make a common life in which differences in beliefs and values could be accepted. Hyper-liberals reject such compromises. Embracing Carl Schmitt's theory that politics is mortal combat between friends and enemies, they extend politics to include all human inter-actions. It is not enough for avowed enemies to be defeated. Hidden heretics must be hunted out, tormented and destroyed. The opportunity for persecution is one of the attractions of hyper-liberalism. 'A scapegoat is named, a festival is declared, the laws are suspended: who would not flock to see the entertainment?'[14]

A contrast may be useful. From some time in the eighth cen-tury of the Christian era, monasteries in Tibet established a practice of debate on the doctrines of Buddhism, which flour-ished widely until the Chinese invaded the country in 1950. The debates, which had some of the qualities of a tournament, inculcated rigour and suppleness in thinking, along with respect for opponents. The ability of medieval Tibetan monks to joust over the intellectual foundations of their society was a sign of high civilization. The inquisitions staged on Western campuses are a mark of advancing barbarism.

The concept of decline has been cancelled from the West-ern lexicon. If it is allowed at all, it is only as a pedagogic device signifying a history that can be corrected. Signs of decay are hailed as progress, disasters as learning experiences that augur a better future.

The belief of some conservatives that woke movements represent a reversion to paganism is the opposite of the truth. Nothing is more foreign to woke sensibility than the extreme moral modesty of pagan religions and philosophies. Like the Enlightenment, which projected a heavenly city on earth, hyper-liberalism is a vehicle for Christian hopes of a new world.[15] Beginning with Augustine, Christian thinkers transformed eschatological expectations of an end-time into a theology in which time and eternity co-exist. Yet Christianity never renounced the hope that the downtrodden of the world would be raised to salvation in heaven.

Pagan religion and philosophy offered no such hope. Wisdom lay in accepting the world. Epicurus was content to enjoy life in a secluded garden when most of humankind was struggling for survival. The Stoic philosopher-emperor Marcus Aurelius looked for peace of mind by playing the part he had been assigned by the cosmos.

E. R. Dodds, one of the greatest twentieth-century classical scholars, identified four advantages of Christianity over paganism:

In the first place, its very exclusiveness, its refusal to concede any value to alternative forms of worship, which is nowadays often felt to be a weakness, was in the circumstances of the time a source of strength . . . There were too many cults, too many mysteries, too many philosophies of life to choose from . . . Christianity made a clean sweep. It lifted the burden of freedom from the shoulders of the individual: one choice, one irrevocable choice, and the road to salvation was clear . . . in an age of anxiety, any 'totalist' creed exerts a powerful attraction: one has only to think of the appeal of communism to many bewildered minds in our own day.

Secondly, Christianity was open to all. In principle, it made no social distinctions; it accepted the manual worker, the slave, the outcast, the ex-criminal . . .

Thirdly . . . Christianity held out to the disinherited the conditional promise of a better inheritance in another world . . . it was also a religion of lively hope . . . Porphyry remarked, as others have done since, that only sick souls stand in need of Christianity. But sick souls were numerous . . .

. . . lastly, the benefits of becoming a Christian were not confined to the next world . . . The Church provided the essentials of social security: it cared for widows and orphans, the old, the unemployed, and the disabled; it provided a burial fund for the poor and a nursing service in time of plague.[16]

These features of Christianity gave it some key advantages in coping with the plagues that ravaged the Roman world. Pagan religion offered scant consolation to those facing a senseless cataclysm in which their way of life was perishing. The gods were indifferent to the sufferings of humans, and what came after death was uncertain. For Christians, plagues were sent by God to test their faith. Believers were enjoined to help one another to live through the trial while preparing for life everlasting.

A combination of psychological and social benefits with differential survival rates helps explain the spread of Christianity. A marginal movement led by a charismatic Jewish prophet was propelled by pestilence into becoming a world religion. An American scholar has written:

The epidemics swamped the explanatory and comforting capacities of paganism and of Hellenic philosophies. In comparison,

Christianity offered a much more satisfactory account of why these terrible times had fallen on humanity, and it projected a hopeful, even enthusiastic, portrait of the future . . .

. . . When disasters struck, the Christians were better able to cope, and this resulted in *substantially higher rates of survival*. This meant that in the aftermath of each epidemic, Christians made up a larger percentage of the population even without new converts . . .

. . . As mortality mounted during each of these epidemics, large numbers of people, especially pagans, would have *lost the bonds* that once might have restrained them from becoming Christians . . . In this way, very substantial numbers of pagans would have been shifted from mainly pagan to mainly Christian networks.[17]

The Christian religion is an accident of history. The historical Jesus, 'the Galilean *hasid* or holy man',[18] addressed his message not to all of humankind but to other Jews. His transformation into a saviour of humankind began with Pontius Pilate. If the Roman governor of Judea had released him under the protection of imperial legionaries, the Jewish prophet might have died at a great age, revered for his contribution to Jewish tradition.[19] (The accidental origins of Christianity, of course, prove nothing. For a believer, chance is the work of providence.)

After Christianity became the religion of the Roman empire, pagan communities lingered on into the seventh century and later, but they were shadows of a vanished world:

The 'final pagan generation' . . . is made up of the last group of elite Romans, both pagan and Christian, who were born into a world in which most people believed that the pagan public religious order of the past few millennia would continue indefinitely. They . . . simply could not imagine a Roman world dominated by a Christian majority . . .

. . . The empire of the first decades of the fourth century contained millions of religious structures, artifacts, and materials that cities and individuals had fashioned over the past millennia to honor the traditional gods. Festivals honoring the gods crowded the calendar, and fragrant smells connected to their worship filled the air of cities. The gods were everywhere in the early fourth century.[20]

Western elites are renouncing tolerance in much the same way pagan elites abandoned their old gods. If the process continues, liberal freedoms will soon be forgotten, along with the world in which they were practised.

Warring rights

Force, and fraud, are in war the two cardinal virtues.

Leviathan, Chapter 13

It seemed clear to one observer, writing in 1989, that the American experiment in rights-based liberalism was heading for a fall:

In the United States . . . every moral and political dispute is cast in the legalistic idiom of rights discourse. Accordingly, the courts, and for that matter the entire procedure of judicial review, have become theatres of doctrinal conflict . . . Litigation substitutes for political reasoning, and the matrix of conventions, subterfuges, and countervailing powers on which any civil society must stand are weakened or distorted . . .

[by] the political self-assertion of collective identities, each of
which seeks privileges and entitlements which cannot in their
nature be extended to all ... it is not hard to see the United
States as heading for an Argentine-style nemesis, in which economic weakness, over-extended government and doctrinal
excess compound with each other to lay waste the inheritance
of civility.[21]

The same observer, writing in 1992, suggested that the nemesis
might come via conflict over abortion:

If the theoretical goal of the new liberalism is the supplanting
of politics by law, its practical result – especially in the United
States ... – has been the emptying of political life of substantive
argument and the political corruption of law. Issues, such as
abortion, that in many other countries have been resolved by a
legislative settlement that involves compromises and which is
known to be politically renegotiable, are in the legalist culture
of the United States matters ... that are intractably contested
and which threaten to become enemies of civil peace.[22]

The new liberalism to which I referred was articulated in the
writings of the American philosophers John Rawls and Ronald
Dworkin. The details of their philosophies have little interest.
Rights-based liberalism is as remote from twenty-first-century
realities as medieval political theory, if not more so.

History has passed by any idea that law can insulate liberal
values from political contestation. A bill of rights may be
useful in codifying liberties and entitlements, but it will
be viable only insofar as it expresses values that are widely
shared in society. When there are deep and abiding ethical
divisions, rights are overturned by the political capture of the

judiciary. After decades of activism by 'right-to-life' groups, this has been the result in America. The next stage, no less predictable, is a breakdown of law.

Liberal rights are political projects promoted by the use of state power. Westward expansion in the United States involved assaults on indigenous peoples that at times are hard to distinguish from genocide. Market capitalism did not emerge spontaneously, in a process of voluntary exchange, from feudalism. The free market was a construction of the state, which enclosed common land and expropriated smallholders.[23] In being imposed from above on recalcitrant populations, nineteenth-century capitalism had much in common with twentieth-century communism. As Hobbes wrote in the Conclusion of *Leviathan*, 'there is scarce a Commonwealth in the world, whose beginnings can in conscience be justified.'

Liberal legalism aimed to replace politics by the adjudication of rights. But, whereas politics can never be a branch of law, law can become a branch of politics. Conflicts of rights reflect divergent understandings of the human good, which cannot be resolved by legal arbitration. Abortion is one such conflict. Attempting to de-politicize the issue politicizes law and turns politics into a mode of warfare.

When *Roe v Wade* – the 1973 Supreme Court decision ruling that the American Constitution protects a woman's freedom to have an abortion – was revoked in June 2022, around two dozen states prohibited the practice, some of them in cases of rape and incest, while exposing doctors and health workers who facilitate the procedure to criminal charges. The Court is not prohibiting abortion. It is devolving the issue to Congress and state legislatures. But conservative judges may go on to challenge contraception and same-sex marriage as well. A moral counter-revolution is being mounted by means of the political capture of the American judicial system.

A school of anti-liberal 'integralism'[24] welcomes this move. The foundations of the American regime are in the Christian religion. The last church to have a special relationship with the state, the Congregationalist Church in Massachusetts, was disestablished in 1833. Yet Christian values continue to be widely authoritative if not often practised. When these values are unmoored from their theological matrix, they become inordinate and extreme. Society descends into a state of moral warfare unrestrained by the Christian insight into human imperfection.

Liberalism is self-undermining in precisely this way, but the vision of an American integralist regime is chimerical. Several European democracies have established churches. In Denmark, Finland, Spain, Austria and Portugal there is a more or less formal marriage between the state and a particular church. The British state contains two established churches – the Anglican Church of England and the Presbyterian Church in Scotland. All these countries are less divided by issues originating in religious belief than the US.

In America at the present time, an attempt at unifying church and state can only heighten divisions. Any such project would be resisted at many levels of government. Awash with guns and with large numbers ready to use them, the country could slide into a chronic condition of low-intensity civil war. The US would be a semi-failed state possessing formidable military capabilities and leading in some advanced technologies, but consumed by internecine doctrinal enmities.

Whether the Supreme Court's judgment on Roe was legally correct is unimportant. Whatever it decided could not end conflict over abortion. Framed as a contest between rights to life and choice, the dispute is irresolvable. If one wins, the other loses. In the US, neither side is ready to concede defeat.

Whether the Constitution gives any guidance on abortion is questionable. Even if it does, the Constitution's authority is strictly local. Rawls and Dworkin aim to show that American jurisprudence presupposes liberal rights. But of what interest is such a deduction beyond American shores? Without some foundation beyond American history and practice, liberal legalism is Lockeanism in one country – a country that is profoundly divided.[25]

Locke's philosophy of rights begins with a theological proposition: human beings are God's property.[26] Contrary to a legend propagated by the libertarian Robert Nozick,[27] there is no right of self-ownership in Locke, who wrote in the *Second Treatise of Government*, Section 6:

> ∴ . . for men being all the Workmanship of one omnipotent and infinitely wise Maker; all the servants of one Sovereign Master, sent in to the world by his order and about his business, they are his property, whose workmanship they are, made to last during his, not one another's pleasure . . .

Locke's belief that human beings belong to God precludes any right to abortion or to suicide. In his *Essay Concerning Human Understanding* (Book I, Chapter 3, Section 19), where he described abortion as one of the most immoral acts, Locke argued that human beings have an immortal soul that belongs to its Creator. The lives of human beings are not theirs to begin or end.

Against this view, Hobbes asserted that women have dominion over their bodies and therefore over their offspring. In *De Cive*, Chapter 9, he wrote:

... Amazons have in former times waged war against their adversaries, and disposed of their children of their own wills, and at this day in diverse places, women are invested with the principal authority ... the child is therefore his whose the mother will have it, and therefore hers; wherefore original dominion over children belongs to the Mother ...

Hobbesian logic does not require accepting any particular view of abortion, even Hobbes's. The goal is not agreement, but modus vivendi.[28] A legal framework governing abortion can only be reached by a political settlement, periodically renegotiated. The same applies to issues around assisted dying, sexuality and gender. When society is divided on such questions, the attempt to resolve them by inventing and enforcing rights is fatal to peace.

Feudalism and fentanyl

To be saved, is to be secured, either respectively, against special evils, or absolutely, against all evil, comprehending Want, Sickness, and Death itself.

Leviathan, Chapter 38

According to the American social theorist Joel Kotkin, a feudal social order is being rebuilt:

Feudalism is making a comeback, long after it was believed to have been deposited in the historical dustbin ... What we are seeing is a new form of aristocracy in the United States and beyond, as wealth in our post-industrial economy is concentrated in fewer hands. Societies are becoming more stratified, with decreasing chances of upward mobility for most of the population. A class of thought leaders and opinion makers, which I call the 'clerisy', provide support for the emerging hierarchy. As avenues for upward social mobility are diminishing, the model of liberal capitalism is losing appeal around the globe, and new doctrines are arising in its place, including ones that lend support to a kind of neo-feudalism.[29]

Many twenty-first-century societies exhibit some of the features of medieval feudalism. Inequalities of wealth and opportunity have increased, while mobility between classes or castes has declined. An intellectual clerisy that justifies these hierarchies is also a reality. But this is not a new kind of medievalism. No modern society has the cultural resources that are needed to reinvent a feudal order.

Feudal societies conferred benefits on their subordinate populations that contemporary societies cannot provide. In return for their labour, serfs were promised protection by lords. Twenty-first-century serfs are abandoned to anarchy and despair. Feudalism was supported by myths of a divine order in which the poorest had a place. The twenty-first-century underclass are offered no place in any scheme of things. Like the 'former persons' of twentieth-century communist regimes, they are retrograde specimens of humanity on the wrong side of history.

In her study of fourteenth-century Europe, Barbara Tuchman observed:

From ownership of land and revenues the noble derived the right to exercise authority over all non-nobles of his territory except the clergy and except merchants who were citizens of a free town. The *grand seigneur*'s authority extended to 'high justice,' meaning the power of life or death, while the lesser

knight's was limited to prison, flogging, and other punish-
ments of 'low justice.' Its basis and justification remained the
duty to protect, as embodied in the lord's oath to his vassals,
which was as binding in theory as theirs to him – and theirs
was binding 'only so long as the lord keeps his oath.' Medieval
political structure was ideally a contract exchanging service
and loyalty in return for protection, justice and order.[30]

Medieval serfs knew their rulers were corrupt:

> Money could buy any kind of dispensation: to legitimize chil-
> dren, of which the majority were those of priests and prelates;
> to divide corpses for the favorite custom of burial in two or
> more places; to permit nuns to keep two maids; to permit a
> converted Jew to visit his unconverted parents; to marry within
> the prohibited degree of consanguinity (with a sliding scale of
> fees for the second, third, and fourth degrees); to trade with an
> infidel Moslem (with a fee required for each ship on a scale
> according to cargo); to receive stolen goods up to a specific
> value. The collection and accounting of all these sums, largely
> handled through Italian bankers, made the physical counting
> of cash a common sight in the papal palace. Whenever he
> entered there, reported Alvar Pelayo, a Spanish official of
> the Curia, 'I found brokers and clergy engaged in reckoning
> the money which lay in heaps before them.'[31]

Millenarian movements rebelled against this ubiquitous corruption. For the most part, though, the population accepted a
myth in which the Church held the key to salvation. Feudal
societies could not save their subjects from sickness, want or
death, but they could promise salvation from these evils in

another life. Contemporary capitalism promises its labourers a better life on earth in a mythical future in which no one any longer believes. In feudal societies, serfs were drugged into acquiescence by a spiritual opiate. In the most advanced liberal society, the underclass die of fentanyl.

Since the year 2000, over a million Americans have died of drug overdoses, most of them involving opioids. The epidemic seems to have begun with over-prescription of painkillers by doctors, who were given financial incentives to prescribe the drugs, but it evinces a more systemic dysfunction. 'Deaths of despair' are an integral part of an economic system in which human labour is treated as a disposable cost of doing business: 'The fundamental cause of that epidemic [of deaths of despair] . . . was not economic fluctuations, but rather the long-term loss of a way of life among white working class Americans.'[32]

This loss of a way of life was one of the causes of the rise from 2016 onwards of 'populism'. The term has no clear meaning, but it is used by liberals to refer to political blowback against the social disruption produced by their own policies. Writing in Moscow in 1918, the soon-to-be exiled Nicolai Berdyaev commented on the distance between the Russian intelligentsia and the rest of society in the run-up to the Revolution: 'The gulf between intelligentsia and "people" was widened, a *national* consciousness became impossible, and only the notion of *populism* remained.'[33] Better than any political scientist, the Orthodox theologian understood that mass movements are often reactions against the hubris of radical elites.

In contemporary capitalism, the underclass and widening sections of the former middle classes are not only exposed

to destitution. They are denied any hope. Capitalism has legit-
imated itself through a myth of unending economic growth.
Now, with pandemics and quickening climate change, this
myth is no longer sustainable. With its disappearance, the
losers in society are left with nothing.

The mythos of Cthulhu

> When the *fairies* are displeased with anybody, they are said to
> send their elves, to pinch them.
>
> *Leviathan*, Chapter 47

A twentieth-century writer on the fringes of literature testifies
to the difficulties of making new myths that assure some kind
of cosmic meaning to humankind in an age of science:

> We live on a placid island of ignorance in the midst of black
> seas of infinity, and it was not meant that we should voyage far.
> The sciences, each straining in its own direction, have hitherto
> harmed us little; but some day the piecing together of dissoci-
> ated knowledge will open up such terrifying vistas of reality,
> and of our frightful position therein, that we shall either go
> mad from the revelation or flee from the deadly light into the
> peace and safety of a new dark age.[34]

The author of these observations struggled himself to find
meaning in life. Born in Providence, Rhode Island, H. P. Lovecraft (1890–1937) was three years old when his father had a
breakdown, probably linked to advancing syphilis, and was
confined in a psychiatric institution, where he died five years
later. Lovecraft's mother, with whom he formed what may

have been his deepest relationship, suffered from anxiety and, after years of mental illness, spent time in the same hospital, where in May 1921 she too died.

A few weeks later he met Sonia Craft Greene, a Ukrainian Jewish widow seven years older than himself, whom he married in 1924. The marriage seems not to have been unhappy. They had shared interests – as well as being a milliner, Sonia was a publisher and pulp-fiction writer – but they drifted apart and soon led separate lives. Sonia moved to the Midwest, then to California, where she remarried and died in 1972. Lovecraft returned to Providence, where he passed the remainder of his days living with two maiden aunts. Throughout his adult life he was often in penury and at times not far from starvation. When dying of cancer he was convinced that his writings, which had received recognition only by a small circle of friends, would soon be forgotten entirely.

In this Lovecraft was mistaken, but he spent his short, unhappy life on the margins of society. His aunts opposed his marriage, partly from snobbery – they claimed to come from an aristocratic background – and partly from the social anti-Semitism commonplace in the US at the time. Estranged from his world, Lovecraft's hatreds ran deep. Believing America was suffering from racial degeneration, he hated the 'polyglot abyss' of New York, and in his letters expressed prejudice against Jews, African Americans and 'foreigners'.

Fortunately, most of Lovecraft's work has nothing to do with his racism. His true subject was the inhumanity of the cosmos. The accidental spawn of a purposeless universe, the human mind was not equipped for knowledge of the world around it. The ruling myths of his time – monotheism and the belief in a process of evolution to higher levels of consciousness – were shields against reality. Against them,

Lovecraft invented his 'Cthulhu mythos', an alternative world whose denizens looked on humans with pitiless unconcern.

Unlike most myths, which assure human beings of their place in the scheme of things, Lovecraft's took for granted that they had none:

> . . . all my tales are based on the fundamental premise that common human laws and interest and emotions have no validity or significance in the vast cosmos-at-large . . . To achieve the essence of real externality, whether of time or space or dimension, one must forget that such things as organic life, good and evil, love and hate, and all such local attributes of a negligible and temporary race called mankind, have any existence at all . . . when we cross the line to the boundless and hideous unknown – the shadow-haunted Outside – we must remember to leave our humanity and terrestrialism at the threshold.[35]

Far from disappearing, Lovecraft's work has been repeatedly rediscovered. His most notable recent champion is the French novelist Michel Houellebecq. Writing in *H. P. Lovecraft, Against the World, Against Life* (1991), Houellebecq celebrates Lovecraft's departure from accepted standards of style and taste: 'There is something not really literary about Lovecraft's work.'

This may be so, but Lovecraft had many literary influences. Not only Edgar Allan Poe, but the Welsh author of unsettling tales Arthur Machen, the English writer of ghost stories M. R. James and the poet, novelist and short-story writer Walter de la Mare all left a mark. But these precursors only highlight what is distinctive in Lovecraft's work. There is nothing in it of Machen's mystical religiosity, James's nostalgia for Victorian values or de la Mare's sense of the lack of substance of the physical world.

Lovecraft was an uncompromising materialist. Unlike many others, he understood that the effect of materialism is not to exalt the human animal but to show its impotence. Our minds are specks of dust randomly tossed about in the cosmic melee. Forever looking for a secure hold on things, humans are in perpetual free fall, seeing the world at odd angles as we hurtle through the void.

Lovecraft is often dismissed as a misanthropist, but a true misanthrope welcomes the insignificance of humankind. Genuinely inhuman myths have existed in the past. The Aztec God Tezcatlipoca – 'The Lord of the Smoking Mirror', the volcanic glass used for divination – was a pointer to what might lie beyond humankind. In one myth, the god turns into a jaguar and destroys the world.[36]

The mirrors into which modern thinkers gaze transfixed reflect only themselves. Despite urging that humanity be left at the threshold, this was Lovecraft's case. Unable to detach himself from his own misfortune, he invented an all-too-human realm of darkness in order to escape the light of cosmic indifference.

Destruction as the cause of coming into being

The secret thoughts of a man run over all things, holy, profane, clean, obscene, grave, and light, without shame, or blame . . .

Leviathan, Chapter 8

You feel that the enemy is within, its characteristic ardour compels you, with inflexible urgency, to do what you do not want to do; you feel the end, the transient, before which you vainly may attempt to flee to an uncertain future. You might ask: is this all? Is this the high point with nothing more beyond? Consequently, we can inquire what happens to the individual in the presence of sexual activity that justifies such a state of mind.[37]

The opening words of a paper delivered at a meeting of the Vienna Psychoanalytic Society on the evening of 29 November 1911, these remarks formed the preface to a bold theory on the connection of sex to death. The speaker, Sabina Spielrein (1885–1942), one of the first practising female psychoanalysts, proposed that human beings were ruled by two instincts or drives, one of self-preservation aiming to survive as an individual, the other to reproduce the species, and these were necessarily conflicting. Bringing another human being into the world was a creative act; but it involved compromising or destroying the individuality of the progenitors of the new being. Without destruction, nothing could come into being.

Sigmund Freud, who chaired the meeting, argued that humans are driven by the pursuit of pleasure. Spielrein challenged Freud's view. The forces governing human behaviour work beneath the conscious self:

The personal psyche can only desire pleasurable feelings, but the collective psyche teaches us what we desire, what is positively or negatively feeling-toned ... Self-preservation is a 'static' drive because it must protect the individual from foreign influences; preservation of the species is a 'dynamic' drive that strives for change, the resurrection of the individual in a new form. No change can take place without the destruction of the former condition.[38]

Freud and his colleague C. G. Jung adopted a patronizing attitude to the ideas presented by the person they called 'the little
Spielrein girl'.[39] Freud objected that any theory of human
instincts should not be grounded in biology: psychoanalysis
was a free-standing discipline. Jung, to whom Spielrein sent a
draft and then a revised version of the paper, acknowledged
receipt of the latter but did not reply for almost a year. When
he did, he wrote of 'uncanny parallels' between Spielrein's
ideas and his own.

In the summer of 1908, four years after Spielrein had become
his first patient at a Swiss psychiatric hospital, Jung had written
to her confessing he had fallen in love with her. Their relationship became sexual, and she came to want a son by him. In
correspondence with Freud, Jung disparaged Spielrein's ideas
as being symptomatic of the traumatic punishment she had
suffered at the hands of her father. 'Her paper,' he wrote, 'is
heavily weighted with her own complexes.' Freud made a
grudging reference to Spielrein's theory in a footnote to his
essay *Beyond the Pleasure Principle* (1920), where he wrote: 'A
considerable proportion of these speculations have been anticipated by Sabina Spielrein (1912) in an interesting and instructive
paper which, however, is not entirely clear to me.'[40]

Spielrein's work was dismissed and then appropriated by
Jung and Freud, but neither of them fully understood what she
was proposing. The power of her theory lay in synthesizing
ideas in philosophy and literature with the disciplines of psychoanalysis and biology. The result may be speculative, but
must count as one of the first attempts at what later came to be
called evolutionary psychology.

By itself, the idea that sexuality serves the interests of the
species in opposition to those of the individual was not new. In

The World as Will and Representation, Schopenhauer wrote that sexual desire

> . . . is really the invisible central point of all action and conduct, and peeps up everywhere, in spite of all the veils drawn over it. It is the cause of war and the aim and object of peace, the basis of the serious and the aim of the joke, the inexhaustible source of wit, the key to all hints and allusions, and the meaning of all secret signs and suggestions, all unexpressed proposals, and all stolen glances; it is the daily thought and desire of the young and often of the old as well, the hourly thought of the unchaste, and the constantly recurring reverie of the chaste even against their will, the ever ready material for a joke, only because the profoundest seriousness lies at its root. This, however, is the piquant element and the jest of the world, that the principal concern of all men is pursued secretly and ostensibly ignored as much as possible. Indeed, we see it take its seat at every moment as the real and hereditary lord of the world, out of the fulness of its own strength, on the ancestral throne, look down thence with scornful glances, and laugh at the arrangements made to subdue it, to imprison it, or at any rate to restrict it, and if possible to keep it concealed, or indeed so to master it that it appears only as an entirely subordinate and secondary concern of life. But all this agrees with the fact that the sexual impulse is the kernel of the will-to-live . . . It is true that the will-to-live manifests itself primarily as an effort to maintain the individual; yet this is only a stage towards the effort to maintain the species.

Schopenhauer identified the conflict later explored by Spielrein and its consequence, a universal state of delusion:

It is true that the species has a prior, closer, and even greater claim to the individual than has the perishable individuality itself. Yet when the individual is to be active, and even to make sacrifices for the sake of the continuance and constitution of the species, the importance of the matter cannot be made so comprehensible to his intellect, calculated as this is merely for individual ends ... Therefore in such a case, nature can attain her end only by implanting in the individual a certain *delusion*, and by virtue of this, that which in truth is merely a good thing for the species seems to him to be a good thing for himself, so that he serves the species, whereas he is under the delusion that he is serving himself. In this process a mere chimera, which vanishes immediately afterwards, floats before him, and, as motive, takes the place of a reality. This *delusion* is *instinct*.[41]

Alongside the instinct to reproduce, which serves the will to live of the species, Schopenhauer posited an impulse seeking freedom from suffering that finds release in the negation of the will:

Before us there is certainly left only nothing; but that which struggles against this flowing away into nothing, namely our nature, is indeed just the will-to-live which we ourselves are ... instead of the restless pressure and effort; instead of the constant transition from desire to apprehension and from joy to sorrow; instead of the never-satisfied and never-dying hope that constitutes the life-dream of the man who wills, we see that peace that is higher than all reason, that ocean-like calmness of spirit, that deep tranquillity, that unshakable confidence and serenity ... what remains after the complete abolition of the will is, for all who are still full of the will, assuredly nothing. But also conversely, to those in whom the will has turned and denied itself, this very real world of ours with all its suns and galaxies, is – nothing.[42]

Undoubtedly Spielrein read Schopenhauer, but she was not recycling ideas she found in his writings. Instead of asserting that the individual yearned for a deathly nothingness, she argued that risking the survival of the individual was necessary for the furtherance of life.

In *Twilight of the Idols* (1886), Nietzsche attacked the very idea of the will, along with that of the ego:

> The 'inner world' is full of phantoms and false lights; the will is one of them. The will no longer moves anything, consequently no longer explains anything – it merely accompanies events, it can also be absent. The so-called 'motive': another error. Merely a surface phenomenon of consciousness, an accompaniment to an act, which conceals rather than exposes . . . And as for the ego! It has become a fable, a fiction, a play on words . . .[43]

Nietzsche had a forerunner in Hobbes, for whom will and self-hood were also a play on words. Where Nietzsche dug deeper than Hobbes was in perceiving that the sources of human action include a drive to destruction. By Hobbes's own account, reason is only a means of reckoning whereby human beings satisfy their impulses. Humans do not desire the good; the good is whatever they desire. Hobbes had no reason for supposing they cannot desire death.

Sabina Spielrein developed the first theory of a death-wish. She was born in 1885 in a merchant family in Rostov-on-the-Don within the Pale of Settlement – the area in the west of tsarist Russia where Jews were allowed to live. They were excluded from academic life and many public institutions. There were periodic pogroms in neighbouring Ukraine, and massacres of Jews in Rostov in 1905 and 1920. Nevertheless Spielrein's family prospered. Her father studied at the University of Berlin. His three sons completed their education abroad, and became professors under the Soviet system.

At the age of eleven Sabina gained a scholarship at a high school, where she focused on languages and classics. When she was fourteen her grandmother died, and a year later her sister. These bereavements seem to have worsened her mental state, already troubled by her relations with her father, and she began to exhibit psychosomatic symptoms. In 1904 she was sent to Geneva for treatment. After an unsatisfactory stay in another clinic, she was admitted on 17 August to the Burgholzli Hospital near Zurich, diagnosed as suffering from hysteria. Her admission was recorded by Jung, who had been working at the hospital since 1900. By December 1904 he was psychoanalysing her.

Perhaps inevitably, her case became entangled with conflicts in the new discipline. One of the points of divergence was the role of sexuality in personal development, with Freud insisting on its central importance and Jung resisting this claim. Between 1909 and 1923, when she returned to Russia, Sabina was in correspondence with both men. Formulating her ideas in the midst of these controversies, she became a respected member of the international psychoanalytical movement.

Her decision to migrate to Russia may seem puzzling. Financial distress may have been a factor. She wanted to set up a psychoanalytical practice in Berlin, but in early 1923 she wrote that she could not pay the rent of her lodgings or afford a consulting room. There may also have been more personal reasons. In 1912 she married Pavel Sheftel, a doctor from Rostov, with whom she had a daughter, Renata. Sabina's husband left her in 1914 and had a daughter with another woman in Russia. When Sabina arrived, the two resumed their marriage, and she had a second daughter, Eva, in 1926. In 1937, Pavel died of a heart attack.

The key to her migration may have been Sabina's belief that the Soviet system would enable her to advance her work. Her profession was essential to her identity. 'It is my calling,' she wrote. 'My life would have no meaning without it.'[44]

Initially based in Moscow, she served in a State Psycho-analytic Institute established in 1922, lecturing on 'The psychology of unconscious thinking', running a training course on psychoanalysis and treating outpatients. She also worked in a Children's House attached to the Institute, which became 'an experimental laboratory for the production of the new Soviet toddler'.[45] In 1925 the Institute and the Children's House were shut down by the Ministry of Education. Around the same time, Sabina left Moscow for Rostov, where she lived with her husband and worked with children, until that too became impossible. Discreetly, she seems to have continued seeing patients for psychoanalysis.

Sabina's move to the Soviet Union was a fatal misjudgement. From the Bolshevik takeover onwards, the new state aimed to impose a single world-view on society. Any freedom it extended to other ideas was based on an assessment of their political usefulness. By the early thirties psychoanalysis, from seeming to be encouraged or at least tolerated, was effectively prohibited.

In the Great Terror that followed, much of Sabina's family was killed. In 1934, Sabina's brother, Isaac, the leading Soviet exponent of industrial psychology, had his institute and journal closed down. In January 1935 he was arrested on charges of Trotskyism and sentenced to five years of hard labour. Two years later he was rearrested, this time on charges of espionage, and his wife and daughter were expelled from their home. Sentenced to death by firing squad, he was shot and his body dumped into a mass grave. His brothers Jan and Emil were arrested and shot in 1938. Around a thousand people were being shot in the Soviet Union every day.[46] Jan's wife was arrested and imprisoned, while Emile's left for Kazakhstan with her two children. In the same year their father, Nikolai, having seen his three sons killed by a regime to which all of them were loyal, died of an unspecified illness, leaving Sabina his only surviving child.

Sabina must have been living in fear, but seems to have had no inkling of the even more terrible events that were in store. Following the German invasion launched in June 1941, Nazi death squads began killing Jews in what has come to be described as 'the Holocaust-by-bullets'. By the end of that year, some half a million had been murdered. German tanks arrived in Rostov in November 1941, but were driven out by the Red Army after only a week.

In November 1937, Sabina was told by her niece Menikha of the atrocities being perpetrated by the Nazi regime, but refused to believe the reports. She could not accept that the people that had given the world Goethe, Heine and Schiller were capable of such cruelty. Before the Germans re-entered the city, around half of its Jewish population, which by then had been increased by an influx of refugees to some 40,000, managed to leave and escape the massacre that followed. Sabina was among those who remained. Whether she still refused to believe reports of German atrocities cannot be known. She may not have chosen to stay but simply failed to leave in time.

In the interlude between the two German occupations of

the city, the Soviet secret police executed anyone they judged to be collaborators. When the Germans reoccupied the city in July 1942, Jews were instructed to identify themselves and gather at assembly points from which they would be transported to safety. Not everyone believed these assurances, and some committed suicide.

The last sighting of Sabina and her daughters was at a street corner waiting for the trucks that would take them away. When they reached a house at the edge of a nearby ravine, the passengers were stripped of their clothes and any jewellery, watches or money they may have had, marched to trenches that had been dug, shot on their knees or upright, and their bodies tossed into pits that had been dug. Over three months, around 27,000 people were murdered in the ravine, including communists and Red Army soldiers as well as Jews. Psychiatric patients at the city mental hospital were also killed, some of them apparently by asphyxiation in mobile gassing vans.[47]

Spielrein's 'death instinct' was a creative force, which served the cause of life. Her misfortune was to live in a time ruled by another death instinct, more like that theorized by Freud. *Thanatos* – as Freud called the antagonist of *Eros*, the impulse of love – was a drive to destruction, which found satisfaction in death, including that of those it possessed.

Freud's death instinct has been the subject of almost universal derision. Many have condemned it as being unscientific. Many more have rejected it because it implied that human beings are flawed in ways that cannot be eradicated by changes in society. But it is not obvious that Freud meant his account as a scientific theory, or that he was wrong in postulating a destructive impulse within the human psyche. In an exchange with Einstein in 1931–2, Freud acknowledged that his theories 'amount to a species of mythology', while observing that the physical sciences may contain myths of their own.[48]

The real flaw in Freud's theory is that it interprets the death instinct as an inherent tendency to entropy leading to the disappearance of life in all material things, and fails to explain why a death instinct developed in humans alone among living creatures. The American theorist Ernest Becker (1924–74) offered an explanation.[49] The destructive impulse was a reaction to the shock of mortality. Human beings repress their awareness of death by identifying themselves with an idea or a belief, and then killing for it. Destroying other human beings for the sake of an abstraction creates an illusion of escape from the mortality of those that are killed. In this psychoanalytical paradox, mass murder is the most extreme expression of death denial.

Spielrein lived in a time of mass murder. When the 'world of security' that Stefan Zweig recalled[50] was destroyed by the Great War, the Habsburg realm was succeeded by a deadly struggle of nations and classes. As societies broke down into groups defining themselves by antagonistic values, incremental progress became impossible. But projects of progress were not abandoned. They mutated into extreme forms, while moral curbs on how they could be promoted were ignored or rejected. The liquidation of groups judged historically obsolete or less than fully human – Jews and Roma, kulaks and 'former persons' – was accepted as a legitimate means of remaking the world on a more advanced model.

Unknown to Spielrein, servants of these death-dealing ideologies penetrated her circle. Her analyst and lover Jung collaborated with the Nazi regime from the time it took power in 1933 until around 1940. A new chairman of the Berlin Psychoanalytic Institute was appointed, Matthias Göring, a cousin of

Field Marshal Herman Göring, who purged it of Jews. Not long after, Jung gave a series of lectures at the Institute in one of which he stated: 'The Aryan unconscious . . . has a higher potential than the Jewish . . .'[51] By 1941, having concluded that the Nazis were losing the war, Jung was an agent of the American intelligence chief Allen Dulles, providing guidance on Hitler's mental state. After the war – when the horror of the Holocaust could not be denied – the great psychoanalyst wrote in a letter: 'Jews are not so innocent after all – the role played by the intellectual Jews in pre-War Germany would be an interesting object of investigation.'[52] Jews, it seemed to Jung, shared the blame for their extermination by the Nazis.

Another member of Spielrein's milieu had links with the Soviet security services. Max Eitingon (1881–1943), a student of Jung's who became a close friend of Freud, was the brother of Naum (often called Leonid) Eitingon (1899–1981), an officer in the NKVD. Leonid organized the kidnapping by Soviet agents of the White émigré leader General Yevgeny Miller in Paris in 1937, an operation in which Max was implicated. Leonid may have been instrumental in the suspicious death of Leon Trotsky's son in a Paris hospital in 1938. He orchestrated the murder of Trotsky himself in Mexico in August 1940, when Ramon Mercador, the son of Caridad Mercador, a communist Leonid recruited in Spain, planted an ice axe in Trotsky's skull. Leonid was awarded the Order of Lenin by Stalin for his work. Whether Max Eitingon was a knowing accomplice in his brother's work has been a matter of controversy. The case against Max is inconclusive. Against it is the fact that many were captivated by his sweetness, generosity and high intelligence. This, too, is inconclusive.[53]

The Soviet state destroyed human life on a gigantic scale, but it was Nazism that incarnated Freud's drive to destruction.

The Holocaust was a unique crime, for it was wholly defined by death. A logic of extermination was inherent in Nazi ideology from the beginning.[54] Even the theorist of Thanatos could not grasp the extremity of the Nazi project. When they began to burn his books in 1933, Freud commented: 'In the Middle Ages they would have burned me; nowadays they are content with burning my books.' Despite everything, Freud believed in human progress. Dying of cancer in September 1939, he could not know that four of his sisters, who remained in Vienna after he left for London in 1938, were to be murdered in Nazi camps in 1942–3.[55]

In her paper, Spielrein explored links between life and death. She did not perish from any death-wish in herself, but was killed by the death-possessed world around her.

Negative theology, negative anthropology

... because the universe is all, that which is no part of it, is *nothing* ...

Leviathan, Chapter 46

A contemporary of Hobbes, Arnold Geulincx is so little known a figure that scholars cannot even agree on how to pronounce his name. Born in Antwerp in 1624, he is reputed to have been fluent in Latin as a child. Matriculating at Leuven University at the age of sixteen, he went on to study theology and was appointed a junior professor in 1646. He became popular in the university while attracting hostility from fellow academics. In 1657 his enemies mobilized against him and he was deprived of his position. In his experience, he wrote, academic life was one in which 'a thousand tediums must be endured, and which is subject to envy and criticism'.[56] He and his family moved to Leiden, where the university was more open to Cartesian philosophy. After a period of poverty he gained a position there, and in 1667 published the first part of a treatise on ethics. In 1669, along with others at the university, he died of plague.

Geulincx and his work began to slip into oblivion. He was not recorded on a medallion produced by the university in memory of faculty who perished in the plague. There is no extant image of him, and it is not known where he was buried. One of his former disciples waged a long campaign after his death alleging he was a follower of Spinoza, and like him a secret atheist. Geulincx's writings were out of print for nearly 200 years.[57]

That he was so nearly forgotten is partly due to the originality of his work. Cartesian philosophy contained an unresolved problem. How could the mind interact with the body? According to Descartes, the two were different substances. Descartes identified the pineal gland, a tiny organ in the centre of the brain, as the physical seat of the soul, but this did not remove the difficulty. How did the pineal gland interact with the soul?

Geulincx's answer was a version of Occasionalism, the doctrine according to which any interaction between mind and body occurs at the will of God. Other versions had been proposed by the medieval Islamic philosopher Al-Ghazali (1058–1111), and the French Catholic Nicholas Malebranche (1638–1715).

The starting point of Geulincx's philosophy is not Descartes's *cogito* – 'I think, therefore I am' – but *nescio* – 'I do not know':

> I have innumerable modes of thought . . . Therefore I think, and think in innumerable modes. But whether things really are as I think of them, I still do not know.[58]

How I come to act cannot be expressed in words:

> Something is said to be ineffable not because we cannot think
> or speak of it (for this would be nothing, nothing and unthink-
> able being the same) but because we cannot think about or
> encompass with our reason how it is done.[59]

In Descartes's philosophy, how the human mind interacts with
the body cannot be explained. For Geulincx, it is a riddle that
could only be resolved by invoking the mystery of divine intervention. Humans are like other animals, ruled by forces they
cannot comprehend. The difference is that humans can realize
their ignorance.

On this basis, Geulincx fashioned an ethics of absurdity. Not
the absurdity of Camus's self-admiring humanist, who finds a
perverse satisfaction in eternally rolling a stone up a hill.[60] For
Geulincx, humans can do nothing, other than submit to the
unknown forces that move them. Humility – 'the most exalted
of the Cardinal Virtues' – means inspecting oneself, realizing
your impotence and resigning yourself to this condition. Ethics
is grounded in the nothingness of the human subject. Yet nothingness is not mere absence, for, as Geulincx wrote, 'Nothing
is more real than nothing.'[61]

It is not surprising that Geulincx should have appealed to
the greatest twentieth-century literary explorer of absurdity.
Samuel Beckett seems first to have come across Geulincx in
Wilhelm Windleband's *A History of Philosophy* (1901). In January 1936, Beckett began studying Geulincx closely, transcribing
sentences in Latin from a copy of Geulincx's *Ethica* he found in
the library of Trinity College Dublin. The book had been out
of print for 185 years. The first English translation appeared in
2006, along with Beckett's notes.[62]

Echoes of Geulincx recur in many of Beckett's writings. In his first published novel, *Murphy*, he writes: 'In the beautiful Belgo-Latin of Arnold Geulincx: *Ubi nihil vales, ibi nihil velis*. ('Wherein you have no power, therein neither should you will.')[63] The novel contains dozens of allusions to Geulincx's philosophy, and Geulincx's maxim illuminates much of Beckett's work.[64]

Beckett took from the forgotten Flemish theologian a mix of negative theology with negative anthropology, which he encapsulated in *Molloy*:

> What I liked in anthropology was its inexhaustible faculty of negation, its relentless definition of man, as though he were no better than God, in terms of what he is not. But my ideas on this subject were always horribly confused, for my knowledge of men was scant and the meaning of being beyond me.[65]

Like Geulincx, Beckett situated a powerless human subject in an unintelligible world. Where he differed was in not linking the two by divine will. In Geulincx the connection is secured by humankind's 'Pater ineffabilis' (ineffable Father), since 'neither we, nor our bodies, nor anything else, can move something without the cooperation of Him who is the author of motion'.[66] Beckett knew of no such author.

Beckett's account of human action has something in common with that in Heinrich von Kleist's 'The Puppet Theatre', first published in 1810. In the story, the German dramatist seems to suggest that a will-less puppet lives more gracefully than a human being, because the puppet is not cursed with self-awareness.[67] Beckett read Kleist's essay, and in directing his play *Happy Days* tried to imbue Winnie, one of the characters, with what he called 'grace in the Kleistian sense'.[68]

Beckett himself possessed that grace at points in his life. During the Second World War, he initially intended to continue living in France as a neutral alien. When a Jewish friend was murdered he joined the Resistance. He was an active member from the end of 1940 until 1943, when he was betrayed to the Germans and forced to live clandestinely for the rest of the war. These were years of hiding from the Gestapo under a false floor, sleeping in haystacks, criss-crossing the country, at times without money and hungry, as his friends and comrades were killed or committed suicide. For his part in the Resistance, Beckett received the Croix de Guerre, the citation for which was signed by General Charles de Gaulle, and the Médaille de la Résistance. Describing his Resistance activities as 'Boy scout stuff', Beckett wrote of the citation in support of the Médaille, which praised his courage, that it was 'too much. Effusive, flowery – not at all necessary.'[69]

There is no evidence either knew of the other's work, but both Hobbes and Geulincx rejected any idea of human autonomy. In Geulincx, the ground of human action was the ineffable will of God. In Hobbes it was in unknowable matter. Human action was the result of forces of which humans know nothing.

An old casino

. . . every man, especially those that are over-provident, are in a state like to that of Prometheus. For as Prometheus (which, interpreted, is *the prudent man,*) was bound to the hill Caucasus, a place of large prospect, where, an eagle feeding on his liver, devoured in the day, as much as was repaired in the night; so that man, which looks too far before him, in the care of future time, hath his heart all the day long, gnawed by fear of death, poverty or other calamity; and has no repose, nor pause of his anxiety, but in sleep.

Leviathan, Chapter 12

The liberal West is possessed by an idea of freedom. Any curb on human will is condemned as a mode of repression. If human beings inflict harm on others it is because society has injured them. When these injustices have been corrected everyone can live as they please, creating the world in which they wish to live. By a droll necessity, this freedom requires that every aspect of life be monitored and controlled. Language must be purified of any traces of thought-crime. The mind must cease to be a private realm and come under scrutiny for its hidden biases and errors. As Dostoevsky anticipated in *Demons*, the logic of limitless freedom is unlimited despotism.

Hobbes believed human beings need limitation as much as they need freedom. This was the message of Christianity: sinful humankind must live by divine guidance. Before Christianity, the need for restraint was recognized in Greek mythology. Prometheus is rightly chained for his hubris. It is also the lesson of the story of Job, where rebellion against God ends with submission to God's authority.[70]

Often interpreted as a prototypically modern thinker, Hobbes reaffirmed this ancient orthodoxy. Today's liberals dream of unfettered human autonomy. Enterprises such as transhumanism and the technological conquest of death are the inevitable end-point of liberalism once it is has been wrenched from the matrix of theology in which it originated. Unbounded self-determination, however, is a fantasy. Human beings cannot create their lives out of nothing, but they can destroy the life they have and be left with nothing.

Conservative thinkers are fond of talking of the suicide of the West.[71] A spectacle of self-immolation, at once tragic and farcical, is being enacted; but suicide involves a measure of self-awareness of which the contemporary Western mind is incapable. An unconscious death-wish is at work. Any project of reviving the liberal West is like Plato's *Republic* as described by George Santayana, 'a prescription to a diseased old man to become young again and try a second life of superhuman virtue. The old man preferred simply to die.'[72]

Nietzsche was the first to detect a death-wish in the modern West. In *The Birth of Tragedy Out of the Spirit of Music* (1872), he identified Socratism – the belief that reason can bring order into human affairs – as its animating myth. Claiming to know nothing, the Greek sage never doubted that in a realm beyond the visible world reason and goodness were one and the same. Detached from this mystical vision and the monotheism it later informed, Socratism is the true faith of the modern West: science can redeem humankind from evil and tragedy. In reality, science serves whatever impulses drive the human animal, including a passion for destruction.

In *The Birth of Tragedy*, Nietzsche distinguished between the Apollonian forces of reason and the Dionysian energy of life. In Greek mythology, Apollo was the god of music and the sun, Dionysius of dance and the underworld. In a balanced way of life, the two gods complemented one other. The chaos beneath was veiled, but not denied. Today, an Apollonian cult insists that chaos can be overcome through the advance of science. But the power of Dionysius increases with the growth of knowledge, and science is a servant of the reigning madness.

In 'Attempt at Self-Criticism', a new foreword to *The Birth of Tragedy* written in 1886, Nietzsche asked:

Is pessimism *inevitably* the sign of decline, decadence, wayward-ness, of wearied, enfeebled instincts? . . . Is there a pessimism of *strength*? An intellectual predilection for what is hard, terrible, evil, problematic in existence, arising from well-being, over-flowing health, the *abundance* of existence? . . . And on the other hand, that which brought about the death of tragedy: the Soc-ratism of morality, the dialectics, modesty and cheerfulness of theoretical man – could not that very Socratism be a symptom of decline, fatigue, infection and the anarchical dissolution of the instincts? . . . And science itself, our own science – what does all of science mean as a symptom of life? Might the scien-tific approach be nothing but fear, flight from pessimism? A subtle form of self-defence against – *the truth*?'[73]

In *The Genealogy of Morals*, he wrote:

We can no long conceal from ourselves *what* is expressed by all that willing which has taken its direction from the ascetic ideal: this hatred of the human, and even more of the animal, and more still of the material, this horror of the senses, of reason itself, this fear of happiness and beauty, this longing to get away from all appearance, change, becoming, death, wishing, from longing itself – all this means – let us dare to grasp it – *a will to nothingness*, an aversion to life, a rebellion against the most fundamental presuppositions of life; but it is and remains a *will*! . . . man would rather will *nothingness* than *not* will.[74]

Nietzsche believed modern atheists deify humanity in order to preserve the God they have lost. But the German prophet succumbed to the same self-deification. The *Übermensch* was Nietzsche's version of God-building.

The deification of the human animal was as alien to Hobbes's way of thinking as the divinization of power. Leviathan was mortal just as every human being is mortal. There is no final deliverance from the state of nature. This is Hobbes's hidden message, which he never fully accepted himself.

If Leviathan is a human artifice, politics is a necessary art. The task of the age is not to bind the new Leviathans, as was attempted in the late liberal era, but to bring them closer to what Hobbes believed Leviathan could be – a vessel of peaceful co-existence. In recognizing that peace can be achieved in many kinds of regime, Hobbes was a truer liberal than those that came after him. The belief that a single form of rule is best for everyone is itself a kind of tyranny.[75]

'Life,' wrote the greatest twentieth-century poet in the English language, 'is an old casino in a park.'[76] The path to the future runs through the past. Putin's klepto-theocracy may persist after his demise, and, if it does not disintegrate, the Russian state may morph into a steampunk Byzantium with nukes. China may continue as a high-tech Panopticon, or renew itself by becoming once again a multicultural empire. If India can recover the complexity of its traditions, it could reinvent the tolerant empire of Ashoka (*c.* 304–232 BC). The European Union may become an avatar of the late Holy Roman Empire, a faded kaleidoscope of shifting principalities and powers. If it does not blunder into a global war to restore its lost hegemony, the US may drift on, a florid hybrid of fundamentalist sects, woke cults and techno-futurist oligarchs. Much of the world may consist of Leviathans surrounded by ungoverned zones, some of which will never emerge from anarchy. Where it can be achieved, peace is a truce, partial and temporary, between the human animal and itself.

Writing of the white whale, Herman Melville warned:

... the great Leviathan is that one creature in the world which must remain unpainted to the last. True, one portrait may hit the mark much nearer than another, but none can hit it with any very considerable degree of exactness. So there is no earthly way of finding out precisely what the whale really looks like. And the only mode in which you can derive even a tolerable idea of his living contour, is by going a whaling yourself; but by so doing, you run no small risk of being eternally stove and sunk by him. Wherefore, it seems you had best not be too fastidious in your curiosity touching this Leviathan.[77]

The real Leviathan is the human animal. Hobbes believed it was driven by self-preservation: humans go on until the world brings them to a stop. He failed to see that death can come from within. Nothing is more real than the nothingness within human beings. Alone among living creatures, they know their lives are bounded by death. Awareness of their mortality impels them to seek immortality in ideas. Killing for the sake of words gives meaning to their lives. In this they exercise the privilege of absurdity, which cannot be renounced.

There is another way of exercising this privilege. The nothingness within may impel action in the service of life. When Samuel Beckett joined the Resistance after his friend was murdered, he risked death for the sake of the living. It may have been this moment Beckett recalled when he wrote that he

loved the image of old Geulincx, dead young, who left me free, on the black boat of Ulysses, to crawl towards the East, along the deck . . . And from the poop, poring upon the wave, a sadly rejoicing slave, I follow with my eyes the proud and futile wake.[78]

If we go on, it is because we cannot do otherwise. It is life that pulls us on, against the tide, life that steers us into the storm.

Notes

Epigraph

1 Thomas Hobbes, *Leviathan*, Oxford and New York, edited with an Introduction and notes by J. C. A. Gaskin, Oxford University Press, 1996, Chapter 5, 30.

1. The return of Leviathan

1 Michael Oakeshott, *Hobbes on Civil Association*, Oxford, Basil Blackwell, 1975; Leo Strauss, *The Political Philosophy of Hobbes: Its Basis and Genesis*, translated by Elsa M. Sinclair, Chicago, University of Chicago Press, 1952; C. B. Macpherson, *The Political Theory of Possessive Individualism: From Hobbes to Locke*, Oxford, Oxford University Press, 1962.

2 John Gray, *Liberalism*, Milton Keynes, Open University Press, 1986, x.

3 John Aubrey, *Aubrey's Brief Lives*, edited by Oliver Lawson Dick, Harmondsworth, Penguin English Library, 1972, 233–4.

4 Ibid., 234.

5 Ibid., 235.

6 Quoted by Richard Tuck in *Hobbes: A Very Short Introduction*, Oxford, Oxford University Press, 2002, 50.

7 Aubrey, *Aubrey's Brief Lives*, 230.

8 Spinoza's rejection of Aristotle's ethics is discussed in my *Feline Philosophy: Cats and the Meaning of Life*, London, Allen Lane, 2020, 47–58.

9 I criticized globalization in *False Dawn: The Delusions of Global Capitalism*, London, Granta Books, 1998 and 2015.

10 Francis Fukuyama, 'The End of History?', *National Interest*, Number 16, Summer 1989, 3–18.

11 John Gray, 'The End of History – or of Liberalism?', *National Review*, 27 October 1989, 33. Republished unaltered under the title 'The End of History – Again?'; this essay can be read in John Gray, *Gray's Anatomy: Selected Writings*, new edition, London, Penguin Books, 2016, 217–23.

12 Charles Darwin, *Autobiographies*, edited by Michael Neve and Sharon Messenger with an Introduction by Michael Neve, London, Penguin Classics, 2002, 50.

13 I considered Darwin's equivocations regarding evolution in *The Immortalization Commission: The Strange Quest to Cheat Death*, London, Allen Lane, 2011, 39–41.

14 For a personal account of corruption in the higher reaches of Chinese capitalism, see Desmond Shum, *Red Roulette: An Insider's Story of Wealth, Power, Corruption and Vengeance in Today's China*, London, Simon and Schuster, 2021.

15 Isabel van Brughen, 'Putin Appointed "Chief Exorcist"', *Newsweek*, 26 October 2022.

16 Isaac Babel, *1920 Diary*, edited with an Introduction and notes by Carol J. Avins, translated by H. T. Willetts, New Haven and London, Yale University Press, 2002.

17 See John J. Dziak, *Chekisty: A History of the KGB*, New York, Ballantine Books, 1988, 35.

18 Ibid., 191–2.

19 Ibid., 3–4.

20 Cited by Yevgenia Albats, *The State within a State: The KGB and Its Hold on Russia – Past, Present and Future*, translated from the Russian by Catherine A. Fitzpatrick, New York, Farrar Straus Giroux, 1994, 49.

21 Ibid., 43.

22 James Meek, 'Russian Patriarch "was KGB spy"', *Guardian*, 12 February 1999.

23 Tony Halpin, 'Russian Orthodox Church Chooses between "ex-KGB candidates" as Patriarch', *The Times*, 26 January 2009.

24 Nicolas Berdyaev, *The Origin of Russian Communism*, translated from the Russian by R. M. French, London, Geoffrey Bles, 1955, 10.

25 Ibid., 130.

26 Donald A. Lowrie, *Rebellious Prophet: A Biography of Nicolas Berdyaev*, London, Gollancz, 1960, 222.

27 See Nicolas Berdyaev, *Self-Knowledge: An Essay in Autobiography*, San Rafael, Calif., Semantron Press, 2009, 244–6.

28 Nicolas Berdyaev, *The Russian Revolution*, Ann Arbor, University of Michigan Press, 1961, 26.

29 Jack Watling and Nick Reynolds, 'Operation Z: The Death Throes of an Imperial Delusion', London, RUSI Special Report, 22 April 2022, 9, n. 46.

30 Reported in Dina Khapaeva, 'Putin and the Apocalypse', Project Syndicate, 24 January 2019.

31 Reported in the *Moscow Times*, 19 October 2018.

32 Dmitry Adamsky, *Russian Nuclear Orthodoxy: Religion, Politics and Strategy*, Stanford, Stanford University Press, 2019, 1–2.

33 Ibid., 87.

34 Ibid., 158–9.

35 For Surkov's role, see Peter Pomarentsev, *Nothing is True and Everything is Possible*, London, Faber and Faber, 2017.

36 Adamsky, *Russian Nuclear Orthodoxy*, 91–2.

37 Nicolas Berdyaev, *The Russian Idea*, New York, Macmillan Company, 1948, 192.

38 Douglas Smith, *The Russian Job: The Forgotten History of How America Saved the Soviet Union from Famine*, London, Picador, 2019, Chapter 12, 143–52.

39 Antony Beevor, *Russia: Revolution and Civil War 1917–1921*, London, Weidenfeld and Nicolson, 2022, 498.

40 Ryszard Kapuściński, *Imperium*, translated from the Polish by Klara Glowczewska, London, Granta Books, 2007, 135–6.

41 Donald Rayfield, *Stalin and His Hangmen*, London, Penguin Books, 2005, 190.

42 Alexander Zinoviev, *The Reality of Communism*, London, Picador, 1986, 53.

43 Alexi Yurchak, *Everything was Forever, until It was No More: The Last Soviet Generation*, Princeton and Oxford, Princeton University Press, 2013.

44 Astolphe de Custine, *Letters from Russia*, translated by Robin Buss, Introduction by Catherine Merridale, London, Penguin Classics, 2014, viii.

45 Joseph de Maistre, *St Petersburg Dialogues, or Conversations on the Temporal Government of Providence*, edited and translated by Richard Brun, Montreal, McGill-Queens University Press, 1993.

46 Peter Elstsov, *The Long Telegram 2.0: A Neo-Kennanite Approach to Russia*, New York and London, Lexington Books, 2020.

47 I analysed the Western intellectual origins of Islamism in *Al Qaeda and What It Means to be Modern*, London, Faber and Faber, 2004, 2nd edition 2007.

48 Evan Osnos, 'Xi Jinping's Historic Bid at the Communist Party Congress', *New Yorker*, 23 October 2022.

49 Warwick Ball, *The Eurasian Steppe: People, Movement, Ideas*, Edinburgh, Edinburgh University Press, 2021, 223.

50 Simon Leys, *The Burning Forest: Essays on Chinese Culture and Politics*, New York, Henry Holt and Company, 1986, 166–7.

51 See the memoir of the French-Chinese writer Jean Pasqualini, published as Bao Ruo-Wang, *Prisoner of Mao*, Harmondsworth, Penguin Books, 1976.

52 Wang Huning, *America Against America*, 1991, 639, 682. No publisher or place of publication is given. For discussions of Huning's views, see Angela Nagle, *Angela Nagle's Newsletter*, 'America Against America', 12 August 2021, N. S. Lyons, 'The Triumph and Terror of Wang Huning', *Palladium: Governance Futurism*, 11 October 2021, and Chang Che, 'How a Book about America's History Foretold China's Future', *New Yorker*, 21 March 2022.

53 For the vital role of Ukraine and the port of Odessa in the global food chain, see Scott Reynolds Nelson, *Oceans of Grain: How American Wheat Remade the World*, New York, Basic Books, 2022.

54 For an account of the role of climate change and pandemics in the fall of the Roman Empire, see Kyle Harper, *The Fate of Rome: Climate, Disease and the End of an Empire*, Princeton and Oxford, Princeton University Press, 2017.

55 Geoffrey Parker, *The Global Crisis: War, Climate Change and Catastrophe in the Seventeenth Century*, New Haven and London, Yale University Press, 2013, 106.

56 Geoffrey Parker, 'Lessons from the Little Ice Age', *New York Times*, 22 March 2014.

57 James Lovelock, *The Revenge of Gaia: Why the Earth is Fighting Back and How We Can Still Save Humanity*, London, Penguin Books, 2007, Chapter 7.

58 George Dyson, *Darwin among the Machines*, London, Penguin Books, 1997, 6, 13.

59 James Lovelock, *Novacene: The Coming Age of Hyperintelligence*, London, Allen Lane, 2019, 130.

2. Artificial states of nature

1 Putin is quoted in Michel Eltchaninoff, *Inside the Mind of Vladimir Putin*, London, Hurst and Company, 2017, 72.

2 Quoted in Glenn Cronin, *Disenchanted Wanderer: The Apocalyptic Vision of Konstantin Leontiev*, Ithaca and London, Northern Illinois University Press, 2021, 7.

3 Ibid., 113.

4 Ibid., 166.

5 Nicolas Berdyaev, *Leontiev*, translated from the Russian by George Reavey, London, Geoffrey Bles, Centenary Press, 1939, 177.

6 Konstantin Leontiev, *Byzantinism and Slavdom*, translated with an Introduction by K. Benois, 2020, Zvolen, Slovakia, and London, Taxiarch Press, 2.

7 Quoted in Cronin, *Disenchanted Wanderer*, 1.

8 Ibid., 166–7.

9 Konstantin Leontiev, *Against the Current: Selections from the Novels, Essays, Notes and Letters*, edited with an Introduction by George Ivask and translated by George Reavey, New York, Weybright and Talley, 1969, 209, 217.

10 On Leontiev as a revolutionary, see Cronin, *Disenchanted Wanderer*, Chapter 13, 'The Red Tsar'.

11 Ibid., 162.

12 Ibid., 187.

13 Ibid., 167.

14 Ibid., 209.

15 Ibid., 203.

16 Quoted in *Four Faces of Rozanov: Christianity, Sex, Jews and the Russian Revolution*, translated with an Introduction by Spencer E. Roberts, New York, Philosophical Library, 1978, 271.

17 Friedrich Nietzsche, *Twilight of the Idols and The Antichrist*, translated by R. J. Hollingdale, Introduction by Michael Tanner, London, Penguin Classics, 2003, 163.

18 Vasily Rozanov, *The Apocalypse of Our Time and Other Writings*, edited with an Introduction by Robert Payne, translated by

Robert Payne and Nikita Romanoff, New York, Prager Publishers, 1977, 238–9.

19 See Vasily Rozanov, *Dostoevsky and the Legend of the Grand Inquisitor*, translated by Spencer E. Roberts, Ithaca and London, Cornell University Press, 1972.

20 Roberts, *Four Faces of Rozanov*, 3.

21 D. H. Lawrence, *Selected Literary Criticism*, edited by Anthony Beal, London, Heinemann, 1986, 247.

22 Quoted in Adam Ure, *Vasilii Rozanov and the Creation: The Edenic Vision and the Rejection of Eschatology*, London and New York, Bloomsbury, 2011, 217.

23 Berdyaev, *Origin of Russian Communism*, 49.

24 See Steven Pinker, *Rationality: What It is, Why It Seems Scarce, Why It Matters*, London, Penguin Books, 2021.

25 Rozanov, *Apocalypse of Our Time*, 228.

26 Ibid., 16.

27 Quoted in Roberts in *Four Faces of Rozanov*, 15.

28 Roberts, *Four Faces of Rozanov*, 278–9.

29 Quoted in Renato Poggioli, *Rozanov*, London, Bowes and Bowes, 1962, 53.

30 Rozanov, *Apocalypse of Our Time*, 274.

31 Ibid., 169.

32 Lesley Chamberlain, *The Philosophy Steamer: Lenin and the Exile of the Intelligentsia*, London, Atlantic Books, 2007, Chapter 5.

33 I explored similarities between medieval millenarianism and modern revolutionary ideologies, including American neoconservatism, in *Black Mass: Apocalyptic Religion and the Death of Utopia*, London, Allen Lane, 2007.

34 Norman Cohn, *The Pursuit of the Millennium: Revolutionary Millenarians and Mystical anarchists of the Middle Ages*, Oxford and New York, Oxford University Press, 1957, revised and expanded in

1970, 148–9. For another perspective, see Richard Landes, *Heaven on Earth: the Varieties of the Millennial Experience*, Oxford and New York, Oxford University Press, 2011.

35 For Lunacharsky's life and impact on Soviet culture, see Sheila Fitzpatrick, *The Commissariat of Enlightenment: Soviet Organization of Education and the Arts under Lunacharsky*, Cambridge, Cambridge University Press, 1970.

36 I discuss the Russian God-builders in *The Immortalization Commission*, London, Allen Lane, 2011, Chapter 2, and Nikolai Federov on pp. 158–60 of that work.

37 I discuss non-humanist varieties of atheism in *Seven Types of Atheism*, London, Allen Lane, 2018, Chapters 6 and 7.

38 Albert Camus, *The Rebel*, London, Penguin Books, 1962, 130.

39 Fyodor Dostoevsky, *Demons*, translated by Richard Pevear and Larissa Volokhonsky, London, Vintage Books, 2006, 402.

40 Ibid., 619.

41 Marx Stirner, *The Ego and Its Own*, edited by David Leopold, Cambridge, Cambridge University Press, 2009, 7. For analyses of Stirner's thought, see R. W. K. Paterson, *The Nihilistic Egoist Max Stirner*, Oxford, Oxford University Press, 1971; John Carroll, *Break-Out from the Crystal Palace: The Anarcho-Psychological Critique*, London, Routledge, 1974 and 2010; and John F. Welsh, *Max Stirner's Dialectical Egoism: A New Interpretation*, Washington DC, Lexington Books, 2010.

42 Fyodor Dostoevsky, *The Brothers Karamazov*, edited by Ralph E. Matlaw, New York, W. W. Norton and Company, 1976, 602, 616.

43 Fyodor Dostoevsky, 'The Dream of a Ridiculous Man', in *A Gentle Creature and Other Stories*, translated by Alan Myers, Oxford, Oxford University Press, 1995, 125.

44 Anna Reid, *Leningrad: Tragedy of a City under Siege, 1941–44*, London, Bloomsbury, 2011, 243.

45 Ibid., 258–9.

46 Alexis Peri, *The War Within: Diaries from the Siege of Leningrad*, Cambridge and London, Harvard University Press, 2017, 145–7.

47 Ibid., 37, 39.

48 *Written in the Dark: Five Poets in the Siege of Leningrad*, edited with an Introduction by Polina Barskova and an Afterword by Ilya Kukulin, New York, Ugly Duckling Press, 2016 and 2018, 39.

49 Ibid., 11.

50 Eugene Lyons, *Assignment in Utopia*, New York, Harcourt, Brace and Company, 1937, 175, 447.

51 Polina Barskova, *Air Raid*, translated from the Russian by Valzhyna Mort, New York, Ugly Duckling Press, 2021, 134.

52 Karl Schlogel, *Moscow, 1937*, translated by Rodney Livingstone, Cambridge, Polity Press, 2012, 1,355.

53 See *I am a Phenomenon Quite Out of the Ordinary: The Notebooks, Diaries and Letters of Daniil Kharms*, selected, translated and edited by Anthony Anemone and Peter Scotto, Boston, Academic Studies Press, 2013, 29.

54 Daniil Kharms, *Russian Absurd: Selected Writings*, Evanston, Northwestern University Press, 2017, 248.

55 Polina Barskova, 'Hair Sticks', in *Living Pictures*, translated from the Russian by Catherine Ciepala, introduction by Eugene Ostashevsky, London, Pushkin Press, 2022, 81–2.

56 Kharms, *Russian Absurd*, 211.

57 Józef Czapski, *Lost Time: Lectures on Proust in a Soviet Prison Camp*, translated by Eric Karpeles, New York, New York Review Books, 2018.

58 Varlam Shalamov, 'Marcel Proust', in *Sketches of the Criminal World: Further Kolyma Stories*, translated by Donald Rayfield, New York, New York Review Books, 2020, 156.

59 Józef Czapksi, *Inhuman Land: Searching for the Truth on Soviet Russia 1941–1942*, translated by Antonia Lloyd-Jones, introduction

by Timothy Snyder, New York, New York Review Books, 2018, 78–9.

60 Józef Czapski, *Memories of Starobielsk: Essays between Art and History*, edited and translated by Alissa Valles, Introduction by Irena Grudzinska Gross, New York, New York Review Books, 2022, 49.

61 Teffi, *Memories: From Moscow to the Black Sea*, translated by Robert Chandler, Elizabeth Chandler, Anne Marie Jackson and Irina Steinberg, London, Pushkin Press, 2016, 63.

62 Teffi, *Rasputin and Other Ironies*, translated by Robert Chandler, Elizabeth Chandler, Rose France and Anne Marie Jackson, London, Pushkin Press, 2016, 106.

63 Nicolas Nabokov, *Bagázh: Memoirs of a Russian Cosmopolitan*, New York, Atheneum, 1975, 142.

64 Teffi, *Rasputin and Other Ironies*, 107.

65 Edythe Haber, *Teffi: A Life of Letters and Laughter*, London and New York, I. B. Tauris, 2019, vi.

66 Adamovich is quoted by Robert Chandler in Teffi, *Memories*, 319–20.

67 J. A. E. Curtis, *The Englishman from Lebedian: A life of Evgeny Zamiatin*, Boston, Academic Studies Press, 2015.

68 Chamberlain, *The Philosophy Steamer*.

69 Arthur Koestler, *Darkness at Noon*, translated by Philip Boehm, edited with an Introduction by Michael Scammel, London and New York, 2019, 241–2.

70 Paul R. Gregory, *Politics, Murder, and Love in Stalin's Kremlin: The Story of Nikolai Bukharin and Anna Larina*, Stanford, Hoover Institution Press, 2010, 142.

71 Aleksander Wat, *My Century*, Foreword by Czesław Miłosz, New York, New York Review Books, 2003.

72 Richard Pipes, *The Unknown Lenin: From the Secret Archives*, New Haven and London, Yale University Press, 1999, 10.

73 Ibid.

74 Isaac Babel, *1920 Diary*, edited with an Introduction and notes by Carol J. Avins, translated by H. T. Willetts, New Haven and London, Yale University Press, 2002, 28.

3. Mortal gods

1 See Peter Turchin, *End Times: Elites, Counter Elites and the Path of Political Disintegration*, London, Allen Lane, 2023.

2 Vilfredo Pareto, *The Rise and Fall of Elites: Application of Theoretical Sociology*, with an Introduction by Hans L. Zetterburg, New Jersey, Transaction Publishers, 1991.

3 For some examples of ideological hiring in American universities, see John Sailer, 'Higher Ed's New Woke Loyalty Oaths', *Tablet*, 22 September 2022. The article links directly to the documents mentioned.

4 BBC News, 27 June 2022, 'World War 2: Memorial to Battle of Bamber Bridge Finished'. A more detailed account of the incident is given by Euell A. Nielsen, 'The Riot of Bamber Bridge (1943)', *Black Past*, 6 July 2020.

5 John Stuart Mill, *Auguste Comte and Positivism*, Ann Arbor, University of Michigan Press, 1973, 136–7.

6 I discussed Mill's proposal of a devil's advocate in *Mill on Liberty: A Defence*, London, Routledge and Kegan Paul, 1983; 2nd edition, London, Taylor and Francis, 2013, 115. See also John Stuart Mill, *On Liberty and Other Essays*, edited with an Introduction by John Gray, Oxford and New York, Oxford University Press, 1991, 26, 43.

7 Mill, *On Liberty and Other Essays,* 139–40.

8 Ibid., 63.

9   Kurt Lampe, *The Birth of Hedonism: The Cyrenaic Philosophers and Pleasure as a Way of Life*, Princeton and Oxford, Princeton University Press, 2015, 54.

10 Mill, *On Liberty and Other Essays*, 15.

11 Ibid., Chapter III.

12 Tom Holland, *Dominion: The Making of the Western Mind*, London, Little Brown, 2019, 601.

13 For the formative role of victimhood in myth, see René Girard, *Things Hidden since the Foundation of the World*, London and New York, Continuum, 2003. The book was first published in French by Éditions Grasset et Fasquelle in 1978.

14 J. M. Coetzee, *Waiting for the Barbarians*, London, Vintage Books, 2004, 131.

15 For the Enlightenment as secular Christianity, see Carl Becker, *The Heavenly City of the Eighteenth-Century Philosophers*, first published 1932, republished New Haven, Yale University Press, 2004.

16 E. R. Dodds, *Pagan and Christian in an Age of Anxiety*, Cambridge, Cambridge University Press, 1965, 133–7.

17 Rodney Stark, *The Rise of Christianity: How the Obscure, Marginal Jesus Movement Became the Dominant Religious Force in the Western World in a Few Centuries*, New York, HarperCollins, 1997, 74–5.

18 Geza Vermes, *Jesus the Jew: A Historian's Reading of the Gospels*, Philadelphia, Fortress Press, 1981, 9. See also Geza Vermes, *The Religion of Jesus the Jew*, Minneapolis, Fortress Press, 1993, Chapters 3, 7.

19 An alternative history, in which a different decision by the Roman governor led to a world without Christianity, is presented by the French Surrealist Roger Caillois in French as *Ponce Pilate*, Paris, Gallimard, 1961, republished as *Pontius Pilate*, introduced by Ivan Lenski and translated by Charles Lam Markman, Charlottesville, University of Virginia Press, 2006.

20 Edward J. Watts, *The Final Pagan Generation: Rome's Unexpected Path to Christianity*, Oakland, University of California Press, 2015, 6, 12.

21 John Gray, 'Hobbes and the Modern State', *The World and I*, March 1989, reprinted in John Gray, *Post-Liberalism: Studies in Political Thought*, London and New York, Routledge, 1993, 14–15.

22 John Gray, 'Against the New Liberalism', *Times Literary Supplement*, 3 July 1992, reprinted in John Gray, *Enlightenment's Wake: Politics and Culture at the Close of the Modern Age*, London and New York, Routledge, 1995, 6.

23 Karl Polanyi, *The Great Transformation: The Political and Economic Origins of Our Time*, Boston, Beacon Press, 2002; first published New York, Farrar and Rinehart, 1944.

24 Patrick Deneen, *Why Liberalism Failed*, New Haven, Yale University Press, 2018. See also Patrick Deneen, *Regime Change: Towards a Post-Liberal Future*, London, Forum Press, 2023.

25 I argued that American liberal legalism was Kantianism in one country in Gray, *Enlightenment's Wake*, 3.

26 See John Dunn, *Locke: A Very Short Introduction*, Oxford, Oxford University Press, 2003, 66–94.

27 Robert Nozick, *Anarchy, State and Utopia*, New York, Basic Books, 1974, 172.

28 For a more extended discussion of modus vivendi, see my book *Two Faces of Liberalism*, Cambridge and Oxford, Polity Press and Blackwell Publishers, 2000, Chapter 4.

29 Joel Kotkin, *The Coming of Neo-Feudalism: A Warning to the Global Middle Class*, New York and London, Encounter Books, 2020, 1.

30 Barbara W. Tuchman, *A Distant Mirror: The Calamitous 14th Century*, New York, Ballantine Books, 1978, 16.

31 Ibid., 27.

32 Anne Case and Angus Deaton, 'United States of Despair', *Project Syndicate*, 15 June 2020. Their research was published in *Deaths of Despair and the Future of Capitalism*, Princeton and Oxford, Princeton University Press, 2020.

33 Nicolas Berdyaev, *Dostoevsky: An Interpretation*, translated by Donald Attwater, Foreword by Boris Jakim, San Rafael, Calif., Semantron Press, 2009, 169.

34 H. P. Lovecraft, *The New Annotated H. P. Lovecraft*, edited with a Foreword and notes by Leslie L. Klinger, New York and London, Liveright Publishing Corporation, 2014, 124.

35 H. P. Lovecraft, *The Call of Cthulhu and Other Weird Stories*, edited with an Introduction and notes by S. T. Joshi, London, Penguin Books, 1999, Introduction.

36 Guilhem Olivier, *Mockeries and Metamorphoses of an Aztec God*, translated by Michael Besson, Boulder, University Press of Colorado, 2003.

37 Sabina Spielrein, 'Destruction as the Cause of Coming into Being', in *Sabina Spielrein: Forgotten Pioneer of Psychoanalysis*, edited by Coline Covington and Barbara Wharton, 2nd edition, London and New York, Routledge, 2015, 186.

38 Ibid., 189, 191, 202.

39 See John Launer, *Sex vs Survival: The life and Ideas of Sabina Spielrein*, London, Duckworth, 2016, 148–9.

40 Ibid., 185. See also John Kerr, *A Dangerous Method: The Story of Jung, Freud and Sabina Spielrein*, London, Atlantic Books, 2012.

41 Arthur Schopenhauer, *The World as Will and Representation*, translated from the German by E. J. F. Payne, vol. II, New York, Dover Publications, 1966, 513–14, 538.

42 Ibid., vol. I, 411–12.

43 Friedrich Nietzsche, *Twilight of the Idols and the Anti-Christ*, translated with an Introduction and a commentary by R. J. Hollingdale, Harmondsworth, Penguin Classics, 1968, 49.

44 Launer, *Sex vs Survival*, 214.

45 Ibid., 221.

46 Ibid., 234.

47 Ibid., 242.

48 'The Einstein–Freud Correspondence, https://www.public.asu
    .edu/~jmlynch/273/documents/FreudEinstein.pdf.

49 Ernest Becker, *The Denial of Death*, New York, The Free Press,
    1973, republished London, Souvenir Press, 2011, 2018. I discuss
    Becker's work in *Feline Philosophy: Cats and the Meaning of Life*,
    London, Penguin Books, 2021, 93–6.

50 Stefan Zweig, *The World of Yesterday: An Autobiography*, Introduc-
    tion by Harry Zohn, Lincoln, Nebr., and London, University of
    Nebraska Press, 1964, Chapter 1.

51 Mark Edmundson, *The Death of Sigmund Freud: Fascism, Psycho-
    analysis and the Rise of Fundamentalism*, London, Bloomsbury,
    2010, 40. I discussed Jung's involvement with Nazism in 'Jung's
    Aryan Unconscious, or What Myths are Not', in *The Silence of
    Animals: On Progress and Other Myths*, London, 2013, 112–18.

52 Cited by Launer, *Sex vs Survival*, 238.

53 For the controversy around Max Eitingon, see Alexander Etkind,
    Eros of the Impossible: The History of Psychoanalysis in Russia, trans-
    lated by Noah and Maria Rubins, London and New York,
    Routledge, 2018, 244–8; Launer, *Sex vs Survival*, 281 fn.6; John
    D. Dziak, *Chekisty*, 112–14; Mary-Kay Wilmers, *The Eitingons: A
    Twentieth-Century Story*, London, Faber and Faber, 2009, 28–9, 34–5,
    181–2. Robert Conquest concluded that Leonid and Max Eitington
    were probably relatives and that 'it seems hard to avoid a case for
    some sort of NKVD connection' between the two. See Robert Con-
    quest, 'Max Eitington, Another View', *New York Times Book Review*,
    3 July 1988, for an authoritative assessment of the evidence.

54 For a psychoanalytical account of Nazi ideology, see Norman
    Cohn, *Warrant for Genocide: The Myth of the Jewish World Con-*

spiracy and the Protocols of the Elders of Zion, New York, Harper and Row, 1966.

55 See Andrew Nagorski, *Saving Freud: A Life in Vienna and an Escape to Freedom in London*, London, Icon Books, 2022.

56 David Tucker, *Samuel Beckett and Arnold Geulincx: Tracing a Literary Fantasia*, London, Bloomsbury, 2012, 10.

57 Ibid., 11–12.

58 Geulincx quoted in ibid., 13.

59 Geulincx quoted in ibid., 15.

60 Albert Camus, *The Myth of Sisyphus and Other Essays*, New York, Alfred A. Knopf, 1955.

61 Geulincx quoted in Tucker, *Samuel Beckett and Arnold Geulincx*, 40.

62 Arnold Geulincx, *Ethics*, with Samuel Beckett's notes, edited by Han van Ruler and Anthony Uhlmann, translated by Martin Wilson, Leiden and Boston, Brill, 2006.

63 Samuel Beckett, *Murphy*, edited by J. C. C. Mays, London, Faber and Faber, 2009, 112.

64 C. J. Ackerley, *Demented Particulars: The Annotated Murphy*, Edinburgh, Edinburgh University Press, 2010.

65 Samuel Beckett, *Three Novels: Molloy, Malone Dies, The Unnamable*, New York, The Grove Press, 2009, 35.

66 Geulincx, quoted in Tucker, *Samuel Beckett and Arnold Geulincx*, 171.

67 I considered Kleist's account of the freedom of puppets in *The Soul of the Marionette: A Short Inquiry into Human Freedom*, London, Penguin Books, 2015, 1–10.

68 Beckett, quoted in Tucker, *Samuel Beckett and Arnold Geulincx*, 170.

69 On Beckett's part in the French Resistance, see Deirdre Bair, *Samuel Beckett: A Biography*, London, Vintage Books, 1990, 320–39.

70 For an argument that the sources of Western civilization are in Homer and the Psalms, see Rachel Bespaloff, *War and the Iliad*,

with essays by Simone Weil and Herman Broch, translated by Mary McCarthy with an Introduction by Christopher Benfey, New York, New York Review Books, 2005, especially Bespaloff's essay 'Poets and Prophets', 87–100.

71 James Burnham, *Suicide of the West: An Essay on the Meaning and Destiny of Liberalism*, with a new Foreword by John O'Sullivan and an Introduction by Roger Kimball, New York and London, Encounter Books, 2014. Formerly the intellectual leader of the American Trotskyist movement, Burnham published this book in 1964.

72 George Santayana, 'Classic Liberty', in *Soliloquies in England and Later Soliloquies*, with an Introduction by Ralph Ross, Ann Arbor, University of Michigan Press, 1967, 166–7.

73 Friedrich Nietzsche, 'Attempt at Self-Criticism', in *The Birth of Tragedy Out of the Spirit of Music*, translated by Shaun Whiteside, edited by Michael Tanner, London, Penguin Classics, 1993, 3, 4.

74 Friedrich Nietzsche, *On the Genealogy of Morals and Ecce Homo*, translated and edited with commentary by Walter Kaufmann, New York, Vintage Books, 1969, 162–3.

75 For an argument that regimes can be better or worse without there being any ideally best regime with which they can be compared, see Gray, *Two Faces of Liberalism*, Chapter 1.

76 Wallace Stevens, 'Academic Discourse at Havana', *The Palm at the End of the Mind: Selected Poems and a Play*, edited by Holly Stevens, New York, Vintage Books, 1960, 86.

77 Herman Melville, *Moby-Dick*, edited with an Introduction and commentary by Harold Beaver, Harmondsworth, Penguin Classics, 1972, 371.

78 Beckett, *Molloy*, in *Three Novels*, 46.

Acknowledgements

I owe to my editor at Penguin, Simon Winder, the opportunity to explore the themes pursued in this book. He suggested I write it, and he has greatly improved my rough text. My agent at the Wylie Agency, Tracy Bohan, gave me unfailing encouragement and advice. Adam Phillips sustained me in the hope that I was pursuing a worthwhile line of thinking. The late Isaiah Berlin stimulated and nurtured my interest in Russian thinkers. All the errors in the book are mine.

Conversations with Bryan Appleyard, Robert Colls, Henry Hardy, David Herman, Gerard Lemos, Michael Lind, Gary Newman, Andy Owen, David Rieff, Paul Schutze, Will Self, James Sherwin, Geoff Smith, Albyn Snowdon and Marcel Theroux have enriched my thinking. Some sections of the book develop ideas tried out in pieces in the *New Statesman*. I am grateful to its editor Jason Cowley and his colleagues Tom Gatti and Gavin Jacobson for giving me the freedom to develop what may at times have seemed contrarian views.

This book began nearly sixty years ago, when I was a pupil in the sixth form of a grammar school in South Shields. A dedicated and inspiring history teacher, Charles Constable, told me to read R. G. Collingwood's *New Leviathan* (1942). My interest in the questions pursued in these pages started with that kindly but compelling instruction.

My greatest debt is to my wife, Mieko, who made this book and so much else possible.

During his academic career, John Gray was a Fellow at Jesus College, University of Oxford; a professor of politics at Oxford; a professor of European thought at the London School of Economics; and a visiting professor at Harvard and Yale. He is the author of more than twenty books that have been translated into more than thirty languages. His recent books include *Straw Dogs: Thoughts on Humans and Other Animals*, *Black Mass: Apocalyptic Religion and the Death of Utopia*, *The Immortalization Commission: Science and the Strange Quest to Cheat Death*, *The Silence of Animals: On Progress and Other Modern Myths*, *The Soul of the Marionette: A Short Inquiry into Human Freedom*, *Seven Types of Atheism*, and *Feline Philosophy: Cats and the Meaning of Life*. He writes regularly for the *New Statesman*.